16130 1

Cooking with Country Ranges

including Aga and Rayburn

CAROL MAY

David & Charles

Frontispiece courtesy of Smallbone of Devizes

AGA and RAYBURN are Trade Marks of the Aga-Rayburn
Division of Glynwed Consumer and Building Products Limited

British Library of Cataloguing in Publication Data

May, Carol
  Cooking with Country Ranges
  including Aga and Rayburn.
  1. Food. Dishes prepared using ranges.
  Recipes
  I. Title
  641.5'8

  ISBN 0-7153-9100-3

First published 1988
Reprinted 1991

© text Carol May 1988
© illustrations David & Charles Publishers plc 1988

Phototypeset by Typesetters (Birmingham) Ltd
and printed in Great Britain
by Butler & Tanner Ltd, Frome
for David & Charles
Brunel House   Newton Abbot   Devon

Contents

Introduction

As a town child I used to look forward to visiting my aunt in the country where the kitchen was warm and welcoming; the memory of the meals she produced from her solid fuel cooker is something which will stay with me for ever. Her enthusiasm for this type of cooker was infectious so I was delighted to find a very old solid fuel cooker in what was to become my home when I married. It took much trial and error to learn how to keep it going once alight and to keep it at a stable temperature without boiling the water in the tank but eventually I found the best way to keep it under control and it became like a member of the family – temperamental at times and on occasions difficult to live with but I wouldn't have been without it!

I now have a large farmhouse kitchen and a more up-to-date model of cooker and I am completely hooked. The kitchen is the hub of my house and the cooker seems to draw people like a magnet as it produces that warm, cosy atmosphere many remember as children. My animals also like the cooker and I often find one of them curled up in front of it.

I have written this book mainly as a guide for those of you who move into a house, find a range type cooker in the kitchen and have little or no idea how to go about using it. I hope the information I have included will help you get the best from your particular appliance, although it is not possible to cover every different model in detail. I have limited my introduction to cover the main cookers on the market – Aga, Rayburn, Esse and Stanley – but the general principles apply to most range type cookers from the Aga through to continental woodburners which provide central heating and hot water as well as cooking. It is, therefore, necessary to contact the manufacturer for detailed instructions, no matter how old the cooker.

Most older cookers are likely to be solid fuel although some will be oil fired, or conversions from solid fuel to oil or gas. Although traditionally thought of as cookers to be found in the country, many are now installed

The Esse Columbian cooker
(Solid Fuel Advisory Board)

in houses and flats in towns and cities, the majority gas-fired.

The recipes have been developed to show the versatility of these cookers and to get away from the idea that they are only used for cooking casseroles. Although they are justly renowned for their slow cooking abilities and the fact that food cooked in them seems to have quite a different flavour, they are capable of cooking anything. The oven shelf position may vary according to the type of cooker and its idiosyncrasies so you will need to experiment to find the best position in your particular case.

As you use your cooker and find that you can use it to cook anything I am sure that you too will become hooked. For those who have been using one of these range types for some time, I hope that this book will provide some new ideas to add to your family favourites.

Range Type Cookers

At the start of the nineteenth century George Bodley, a Devon ironfounder, patented the first cast-iron closed-top cooking range. It not only became the prototype of cooking ranges throughout the rest of the century but was also a landmark in the development of the kitchen; the life of the open hearth was coming to an end. The range had a raised open coal fire flanked by an oven and a water tank, all housed beneath a flat cast-iron hotplate. By the middle of the nineteenth century the forerunner of our modern cooking ranges, the 'kitchener' or closed—in range had been developed, still burning coal and requiring continual attention in the form of refuelling and blackleading.

In the 1920s Dr Gustav Dalen, a Swedish physicist, invented the first heat storage cooker, the Aga. His aim was to design an appliance capable of every cooking method – baking, boiling, braising, frying, grilling, toasting, stewing, roasting, steaming and simmering – while at the same time providing perfect cooking and automatic heat control. Today, the Aga cooker will still do exactly that although it can now be run on oil, gas and electricity as well as solid fuel.

New and recent developments have made a wide choice of range type cookers available, many of which will also heat a system of radiators (an Aga cooker is only designed to cook and heat hot water). These are generally classed as 'insulated' cookers and have a different method of heat control. Most run on coal, wood or peat briquettes, although a few are made to run on oil or gas. Most now have two ovens with a thermostat on the outside of the top, hotter, oven.

Before you use your cooker it is important to understand how it operates in order to get the best results. All the manufacturers produce detailed instruction booklets obtainable from them (addresses on page 16). However, I have included here general principles of operation so that you can at least start using your particular model.

The Aga Cooker

The Aga works on the principle of heat storage – the heat being stored within the body of the cooker in the ovens, the hotplates and the combustion unit (whatever the fuel used) at just the right temperature for immediate use either during the day or overnight. This high degree of internal heat is maintained by minimal consumption of fuel. The hotplate covers and the casing are very well insulated to keep in as much of the heat as possible.

Temperature Control

When the cooker is first installed the thermostat is set on 2 which will normally produce the correct temperature range required as indicated by the position of the mercury in the heat gauge. This should be checked every morning and if the mercury level is consistently low the thermostat control should be turned up by half a notch until the mercury consistently reaches the centre line first thing in the morning or after several hours when no cooking has been done. Once the correct setting has been reached there should be no need to move the control again (see tips on usage when it might be necessary).

The Boiling Plate

When the cooker is up to its optimum temperature, the boiling plate will boil more rapidly than a conventional electric or gas hob. The heat is spread evenly over the whole surface so that 3 or 4 pans can be used at once as they will continue to boil even when making only partial contact with the hotplate. The boiling plate is used for any foods such as vegetables which would normally be cooked quickly in water, for deep frying, steaming and the rapid frying of foods, eg the sealing of meat. Once boiling the pan is transferred to the simmering plate.

Simmering Plate

Situated above the ovens rather than the firebox, the temperature of the simmering plate is much lower than that of the boiling plate; it is therefore ideal for more gentle cooking such as the simmering of vegetables and steamed puddings and the making of sauces. Again, several pans can be placed on the hotplate together. It is important to keep both the insulating lids closed when the hotplates are not in use to conserve the stored heat.

Warming Plate

The 4-oven Aga also has a warming plate which is at a much lower temperature and is useful for keeping foods warm.

Roasting Oven

All of the oven space can be used – even the floor. As with most types of cooker there is a difference in temperature between the top and bottom of the oven and it is this which governs where foods are cooked. For example, foods requiring a hot temperature such as Yorkshire pudding, scones, pastry dishes and grilled foods should be placed near the top of the oven on either the grid shelf, a roasting tin or the solid shelf if cooking another dish at a lower temperature underneath. Small cakes, joints, jacket potatoes and baked dishes are better cooked lower in the oven or sometimes on the floor of the oven, depending on what else is being cooked at the same time. As there is plenty of room to cook several dishes requiring different temperatures at the same time it is possible to cook a complete meal. Two dishes requiring the same temperature can also be cooked together as the oven is deep and the capacity large (I have cooked a 35lb turkey in this oven).

The top heat can be cut off using the cold solid shelf placed on the top set of runners. This is useful when baking many things requiring a more moderate temperature, eg large cakes. The solid shelf can also be used as a baking tray when cooking biscuits, pastries, scones etc, thus cooling the lower half of the oven for baking larger cakes. Bread making is very successful with these cookers, the dough being proved on the insulated lids and baked in the centre of the roasting oven.

Simmering Oven

This is a slow cooking oven for casseroles, custards, fish, vegetables and low-temperature cake baking. A complete meal can be left in quite happily to cook all day without drying out. Steamed puddings can be cooked in this oven after initial steaming on the hotplates and it is also very good for porridge, left to cook gently overnight. All the foods must initially be brought to the boil, or at least a normal cooking temperature, on another part of the cooker. Stock is made economically by using the simmering oven and of course excellent fruit cakes and meringues are cooked in this slow heat. After 2 hours in the simmering oven meringues can be placed on a tea towel on the insulated lid above the simmering plate to finish off. The whole oven can be used for warming plates and for keeping food hot without drying out.

The Baking Oven

The 4-oven Aga also has a baking oven and a plate-warming oven. Like the roasting oven the baking oven has several temperature zones but it operates at a lower temperature range. The top of the oven is ideal for baking foods such as small cakes, the centre of the oven for larger cakes, flans etc, while shortbread, gingerbread, baked cheesecakes and some fruit cakes are baked at the bottom.

The Plate Warming Oven

This oven is used mainly for warming plates and serving dishes and for keeping food hot, although it can be used in the same way as the simmering oven. Both these ovens can be used for warming bread or rolls before serving.

Insulated Cookers

Le Creuset enamelled cast iron (The Kitchenware Merchants Ltd)

These are similar in appearance to the heat-storage type of cooker, the main difference being that they require more work on the part of the cook to obtain the required cooking temperatures. However, because of this and the fact that they are less selective of fuel, they are considered by many to be more flexible. They are run on the principle of maximum insulation to keep the heat generated within the cooker for use.

At night, open the chimney damper, riddle the fire, empty the ashpan and refuel. Close the ashpit door and spinwheel, then open the latter a quarter turn (leave completely closed if burning wood). Close the damper to number 1. For woodburners, open the door on the flue chamber, using whichever method is provided on the cooker (lever or wheel usually), to minimise the burning rate and flue condensation. The exact amount can only be determined by experimentation and weather conditions.

In the morning, open the spinwheel and damper, riddle and refuel. If the hotplate is required immediately do not refuel until after use.

Fuels

All types of cooker covered in this book are designed to be kept burning overnight and this is the most efficient way of using them. Insulated cookers will burn any of the following range of manufactured and natural smokeless fuels: Phurnacite, Coalite, Sunbrite, Rexco Nuts, Welsh dry steam (small nuts), anthracite stove nuts and Stovesse. House coal, wood and peat briquettes can also be burned efficiently. All these fuels have different calorific values and heating performance will vary accordingly.

Wood has half the calorific value of coal but is easy to light and

provides heat quickly. It should be perfectly dry to obtain the best cooker performance and to minimise creosote deposits in the flueways. 'Green' wood also increases creosote deposits, so leave it to mature for at least one year under cover before use. Wet kitchen refuse should never be burned for the same reason.

Of the smokeless fuels anthracite and Phurnacite have the highest calorific values and give the longest period between refuellings. These fuels are recommended if the cooker is expected to provide hot water and full central heating as well as cooking facilities. To fuel a cooker expected to do all that work on wood alone would involve someone in almost constant stoking and tending.

The solid-fuel Aga cooker is designed to burn Phurnacite, anthracite stove nuts and Sunbrite doubles only; none of the other fuels mentioned above are suitable and neither is wood or peat. Again, all fuels should be stored under cover.

Oil-fired cookers of both types are designed to burn commercial kerosene, otherwise known as 28–second oil. Although 35-second oil is also available, this will smoke badly and is not recommended. Gas-fired cookers have burners suitable for either natural gas or bottled gas, otherwise known as LPG.

Electric Agas are the latest addition to the range and run solely on Economy 7 overnight electricity. If necessary they will take a boost on Economy 7 day rate.

Cleaning and Care

The vitreous enamel surfaces are easily cleaned with a damp cloth dipped in hot soapy water, and can then be buffed up with a clean dry cloth. The area round the hotplates should be wiped clean after cooking to prevent spills sticking to the surface and becoming more difficult to clean. Insulated cookers can be allowed to cool down a little before cleaning. Milk and acid foods such as fruit juice should be wiped off immediately to prevent discolouration or damage to the enamel.

The linings of the lid over the boiling plate can be considered as self cleaning. However, the lining of the lid over the simmering plate and the insides of the oven doors may be cleaned with wire wool and soapy water. Open the lid to allow it to cool a little first. The oven doors are removable but never be tempted to immerse them in water as this will damage the insulating-material inside them. The hotplates themselves are cleaned with a wire brush.

The roasting and baking ovens are also considered self cleaning and merely need brushing out occasionally with a stiff brush. The simmering and plate warming ovens may also need wiping out with a damp soapy cloth. Clean the grid and solid shelves regularly to prevent food spills and grease building up. Soak first to make cleaning easier, then use any type of abrasive cleaner.

Flue Cleaning

The manufacturer's instruction booklet will give detailed information on cleaning the flues on your particular model. However, generally speaking the flueways should be cleaned out once a month using the tools provided. If wood is used, this may need to be done weekly. Inspect the soot box at the base of the chimney every 3 months (monthly if burning wood) and remove any accumulation of sooty deposits. The chimney should be swept annually, although it may need to be done every 3–4 months with wood burners.

Service

Solid fuel and gas-fired Aga cookers should be serviced annually by an authorised Aga distributor. Oil-fired cookers should be inspected and cleaned at roughly six monthly intervals. Any oil- or gas-fired insulated cooker will also need regular servicing to check the burner.

With all types of solid fuel cooker it is necessary to check the grate regularly for signs of fractures. Also check the firebricks in an insulated cooker for cracks. Any problems with the barrel in an Aga cooker will show up if the cooker is regularly serviced.

Useful Addresses

Glynwed Appliances Ltd, PO Box 30, Ketley, Telford, Shropshire, TF1 1BR.
Manufactures both the Aga and Rayburn cookers.
Smith & Wellstood Ltd, Bonnybridge, Stirlingshire, Scotland, FK4 2AP.
Manufactures the Esse range of cookers.
Calfire (Chirk) Ltd, Unit One, Acorn Industrial Estate, Holyhead Road, Chirk, Clwyd, LL14 5NA
Imports and distributes Stanley cookers.
The Solid Fuel Advisory Service, Hobart House, Grosvenor Place, London SW1 or look up the address of your nearest area office in Yellow Pages.

Utensils

To get the best from your cooker it is essential to use utensils with flat machined bases, such as good-quality aluminium or cast-iron oven-to-tableware, on the hotplates. These types of cookware have completely flat bases which withstand distortion and ensure an even spread of heat, even when the pans are making only partial contact with the hotplate. Copper-bottomed pans are to be avoided as they will distort badly with the intense heat. Any type of ovenproof ware can be used in the ovens.

Aga Cakebaker

Certain specialised pieces of equipment have been produced by some manufacturers, one of the best known being the Aga cakebaker. It is basically an ovenproof saucepan containing a metal trivet and several cake tins and is used to protect cakes requiring a lower temperature for more than 45 minutes from the heat of the roasting oven. Put the pan in the oven to warm up while making the cake then just pop the cake tin on the rivet inside, cover and cook for the required time.

It is possible to make up your own cakebaker using an aluminium ovenproof stewpan with heatproof handles and a metal trivet of some

sort. However, make sure that the trivet is wider than the cake tin if a loose-bottomed tin is used or it will push the cake mixture out of the tin!

Aga Toaster

The Aga toaster is supplied with the cooker and can be used for both toast and toasted sandwiches. Heat it on the boiling plate first (this helps to prevent the bread sticking), then arrange slices of bread between the two halves of the toaster. Place on the boiling plate (the lid can be lowered to conserve the heat and maintain good contact, but don't forget about it!) and cook first one side then the other. Melba toast is best made by placing the bread directly on the floor of the roasting oven.

Aga Griller

The Aga griller can be used on any range type of cooker for the cooking of steaks and other thick cuts of meat. Simply place the griller straight onto the boiling plate and leave for 3–4 minutes to get really hot. Place the meat on the ridges and press down lightly. Cook for 2–3 minutes on each side to give a nicely browned outside and juicy centre.

A Few Tips

- Try to use the oven rather than the hob as much as possible to conserve the heat. Many cooking processes can be carried out just as successfully in the oven. Cook vegetables in the oven by bringing to the boil first and then placing either in the roasting or the simmering oven to cook slowly all day. Soups can be left to cook in casseroles or stewpans in the simmering oven, having first softened the ingredients on the top.

- Use the simmering oven to make golden breadcrumbs – simply dry out the bread in it overnight and then crush.

- Use the meat tins to hold dishes or casseroles when the grid shelf is in use elsewhere or when grilling.

- When a member of the family is late in for a meal simply plate up the food, cover with foil and place in the simmering oven to keep warm without drying out.

- The ovens are vented into the flue so most of the cooking smells go up the chimney, not out into the kitchen. It is therefore a good idea to use a kitchen timer to remind you that something is cooking.

- The oven temperature does not drop as soon as you open the doors so it is easy to check on the progress of cooking without affecting the end results.

- If in doubt about the temperature, use an oven thermometer – it will put your mind at ease if the dish requires a particular temperature to give the best results. It will also help you to get used to the temperature zones in the cooker. If the temperature is too high, protect the food with the cold solid shelf and if need be a layer of foil. Place cakes in a cakebaker. Alternatively, close the spinwheel on an insulated cooker and wait for the temperature to drop. Although it will waste heat, the hob covers on an Aga can be lifted up and the temperature will slowly drop.

- The more the cooker is used the more quickly the oven temperature will drop, particularly with heat storage cookers. Batch baking or cooking a meal for a large number of people will cause the oven temperature to drop slowly. When roasting meat this can be an advantage as the meat will quickly become sealed and then cook through more slowly. However, this may lead to the cooker having insufficient heat to cook the vegetables. If this happens often with a heat storage cooker I would suggest turning up the thermostat half a notch 24 hours beforehand to give the oven an extra boost, then turning it down to its normal setting after use.

- Both types of cooker have a reputation for being temperamental but most of this is due to the weather or misuse. A windy day will draw the fire and may cause the cooker to overheat, while a damp foggy day will have a dampening effect. With insulated cookers, where the temperature control is more flexible the temperature can quickly be raised using the spinwheel on the firebox door. With heat-storage cookers, where the temperature is set and would normally take up to 24 hours to alter, the temperature can sometimes be raised by flipping over the plug in the top of the simmering plate and replacing the insulated lid. The temperature will still take several hours to rise. This can also be done if the cooker is in danger of going out and will sometimes increase the air flow sufficiently to keep it going.

- Remember to keep the ashpan emptied regularly to ensure an adequate flow of air to maintain temperature.

- If the cooker is overheating due to excessive wind, lift up the insulated lids and leave them up until the temperature drops to a safe level. With an insulated cooker use the chimney damper to reduce the pull on the fire. Prolonged overheating will break the oven thermometer and could distort the hotplates. Excessive fire temperatures with solid fuel cookers will also cause the fuel to clinker which will damage the grate and the firebricks.

- If excessive draught is a regular problem, causing overheating, it may be necessary to fit a flue stabiliser in the chimney breast above the cooker.

The Aga as the focus of a delightful country kitchen (Smallbone of Devizes)

This draws air from the room, thereby reducing the amount of air drawn through the cooker and preventing overheating.

- Most insulated cookers have easily removable firebricks – the full set is kept in to reduce the size of the firebox for summer use of hot water and limited cooking only. The side bricks are removed for full winter use with central heating. This also means they are easily replaced if they are damaged.

- If the cooker is solid fuel, use the fuel which best suits the cooker, its position and your requirements. Wood will give instant heat but will die down as quickly, while the quality smokeless fuels heat up more slowly but provide a more instant and longer lasting heat. Do not refuel just before you want to cook – all these cookers take time to get up to temperature.

- Cookers which heat hot water and radiators may require extra stoking during periods when the heating is on and hot water is being used, if a usable oven temperature is to be maintained.

- Older models of insulated cookers are often sited next to or directly underneath the hot water tank and during periods of overheating, the water in the tank may boil. Lifting up the hob covers and leaving the fire to die down a bit may be sufficient but if not, run off some of the water for a bath!

- Cookers which have been converted from one fuel to another are unlikely to be as efficient as when fired by the original fuel. With conversions from solid fuel to oil, in particular, the temperature of the simmering plate may be higher than with solid fuel.

- Do not slam shut the oven and firedoors as this will wear away the metal retainer catches – lift them onto the catches instead.

The Recipes

Unless otherwise stated, the recipes are intended to serve 4–6 people. The cooking times are only a guide and will vary according to the cooker and type of dish used.

Metric and imperial measurements have been calculated separately so use only one set of measurements as they are not exact equivalents. All spoon measurements are level.

All eggs are size 2 or 3 unless otherwise stated.

Crème Fraîche

Crème fraîche is a lightly soured cream from France which is now becoming more widely available in large supermarkets. If you are unable to buy it, an alternative can be made by mixing equal quantities of soured cream and lightly whipped whipping cream.

Filo or Strudel Pastry

Filo or strudel pastry is tissue-thin Greek pastry which is available either chilled or frozen from delicatessens and some larger supermarkets. If fresh, it should be stored in the fridge in a plastic bag to prevent it drying out. If frozen, thaw in the packet. It may be re-frozen successfully. When using filo pastry keep it covered with a damp cloth to prevent it drying out. Brushing melted butter between the sheets keeps the layers separate and gives the pastry its characteristic crispness. Margarine or vegetable oil may be used instead, but the flavour is not as good. Filo pastry may be filled with almost anything sweet or savoury and can be made into individual portions by using each sheet separately (see Chicken and Spinach Strudels page 81) or the sheets may be piled one on top of the other and rolled up together to form one large roll (see Plum and Almond Strudel page 78).

Fromage Frais

Fromage frais or fromage blanc also originates from France and is widely available in supermarkets. It usually comes in two or three grades according to the fat content so the higher the fat content the creamier will be the flavour. It is also available flavoured in small pots and has a wide variety of uses. Mixing low fat soft cheese with cream or plain yoghurt will give an acceptable alternative but in most recipes it may be substituted with any type of plain yoghurt, crème fraîche or soured cream.

Passatta

Passatta is smooth, thick, sieved tomatoes which usually comes in a jar and needs refrigeration after opening. Should this not be available, an alternative may be made by puréeing and then sieving a can of tomatoes with the juice.

Breakfast Dishes

Cooked English Breakfast

This is based on a mixture of the following:

sausages
bacon rashers
kidneys
tomatoes
mushrooms
eggs
fried bread

Place the chosen meats in a roasting tin and cook on the floor of the roasting oven for 15–20 minutes. Add halved tomatoes, mushrooms, eggs and slices of bread and continue to cook until eggs are set. Serve immediately.

Apricot and Apple Breakfast Bread

275g (10oz) self-raising wholemeal flour
25g (1oz) sesame seeds
110g (4oz) butter
275g (10oz) lemon curd
3 × 15ml sp (3tbsp) thick natural yoghurt eg: greek style
50g (2oz) no-soak dried apricots, roughly chopped
50g (2oz) dried apples, roughly chopped
50g (2oz) no-soak dried figs, roughly chopped
sliced dried fruits and sesame seeds to decorate
apricot jam to glaze

1   In a large bowl mix together the flour and sesame seeds. Rub in butter until the mixture resembles breadcrumbs.
2   Add the lemon curd and yoghurt followed by the dried fruits.
3   Spoon the mixture into a greased and lined 900g (2lb) loaf tin and level out. Bake at 375°F (190°C) in the centre of the roasting oven on the grid shelf with the cold solid shelf on the top set of runners, or in the baking oven, for 50 minutes to 1 hour. Remove from the oven and leave to cool in the tin.
4   Turn out onto a cooling rack and decorate with slices of dried fruit. Glaze with a little warmed and sieved apricot jam and sprinkle with sesame seeds.
5   To serve, slice and spread with butter or a favourite conserve. This bread will keep in an airtight tin for a week and when dry can be toasted.

Grapefruit Breakfast Bread   *colour below*

1×285g (10½oz) grapefruit
 segments in natural juice
225g (8oz) self-raising wholemeal
 flour
1×5ml sp (1tsp) baking powder
50g (2oz) butter or margarine
50g (2oz) light soft brown sugar
1 egg
75g (3oz) sultanas

1   Strain the grapefruit, reserving the juice. Roughly chop the fruit.
2   Sieve the flour with the baking powder.
3   Cream the butter with the sugar until light and fluffy. Beat in the egg then fold in the flour, sultanas and grapefruit with sufficient juice to make a soft dropping consistency.
4   Place in a greased and lined 900g (2lb) loaf tin and bake at 350°F (180°C) in the centre of the baking oven or on the grid shelf on the base of the roasting oven protected by the cold solid shelf for 45–50 minutes. Allow to cool completely in the tin, before removing.
5   Serve sliced and spread with butter.

Note: This loaf keeps well in an airtight tin.

Scrambled Eggs on Toast

3 eggs
2×15ml sp (2tbsp) milk
salt and pepper
15g (½oz) butter

1   Beat the eggs together with the milk and seasoning.
2   Heat the butter gently in a saucepan on the simmering plate, add the egg mixture and stir continuously with a wooden spoon until just set and creamy.
3   Serve on hot buttered toast (see page 17 for how to make toast using the special Aga toaster).

*Grapefruit Breakfast Bread
(John West Foods Ltd)*

1×15ml sp (1tbsp) clear honey
1×15ml sp (1tbsp) brown sugar
2×5ml sp (2tsp) sunflower oil
few drops vanilla essence
50g (2oz) mixed nuts, chopped

Muesli base:
75g (3oz) rolled oats
15g (½oz) bran
15g (½oz) wheat germ
25g (1oz) bran flakes

Toasted Muesli

1   Put the honey and sugar into a small pan over a low heat until they dissolve. Remove from heat, add the oil, vanilla essence and nuts, then stir in the muesli base.
2   Spread the mixture on a baking tray and bake at 350°F (180°C) or at the bottom of the roasting oven for about 20 minutes, stirring occasionally so that it browns evenly. Allow to cool on the tray.
3   Serve with fresh or dried fruits and more nuts, or as it is with natural yoghurt.

Note: This muesli can be stored in a covered jar.

1 litre (2pt) skimmed milk (or
  the same amount reconstituted
  from powdered skimmed milk
2×5ml sp (2tsp) any plain low-fat
  yoghurt
flavourings: chopped fruits,
  chopped nuts, 3×5ml sp (3tsp)
  cocoa powder or honey

Homemade Yoghurt

1   Scald a 1½ litre (3pt) pudding basin with boiling water to sterilise it.
2   Bring the milk to the boil and let it continue to boil for 2 minutes as this improves the flavour of the finished yoghurt. Pour into the basin and leave until it has cooled to a temperature of 113°F (45°C). If you don't have a thermometer use your finger – the milk should feel slightly hotter than you can comfortably bear. If the milk is too hot at this stage it will destroy the yoghurt culture and the mix will not set.
3   When the milk has reached the correct temperature stir in the plain yoghurt starter. Cover the basin tightly with clingfilm, then quickly wrap it in several layers of insulation – eg three thick towels – and place it on or near the top of the cooker. If the temperature of the cooker is low, the insulated bowl may be placed in the simmering oven with the door ajar.

4 After 5–6 hours the yoghurt should have set. If it is still runny, wrap it up again and leave for another hour. There will be a layer of yellowish whey lying on the surface; carefully pour this off, then immediately transfer the yoghurt to the refrigerator.

Notes: Remember to keep back some of the yoghurt as a starter for the next batch; you should not need to buy any new starter for several months.

The yoghurt can be thickened by straining it for 30 minutes or so through a sieve lined with kitchen paper, or through several layers of muslin.

If the yoghurt fails to set the usual reasons are:
The starter was too stale; use only the freshest yoghurt.
Too much starter results in a sour, grainy yoghurt; do not be tempted to add a little bit more.
The temperature of the milk was too high.
The yoghurt was not kept in a warm enough place or the insulation was not adequate.

Variation:
Yoghurt cheese can be made by extending the straining process (method 5) to 8 hours. This produces a pleasant, slightly acid curd-type cheese.

Porridge

1 Bring the water to the boil, sprinkle in the oats and salt and simmer on the simmering plate for 5 minutes.
2 Cover and leave on the grid shelf on the floor of the simmering oven overnight.

600ml (1pt) water (or mixture of milk and water)
75g (3oz) coarse or medium oatmeal
1×5ml sp (1tsp) salt

Kedgeree

1 Place the haddock fillets in a saucepan and cover with ½ litre (1pt) cold water. Bring to the boil on the boiling plate, put on a lid, and simmer gently on the simmering plate for 8 minutes. Drain off the water into a measuring jug. Transfer the haddock to a dish, cover with foil and keep warm in the simmering oven.
2 Using the same saucepan, melt the butter and soften the onion in it for 5 minutes. Stir in the curry powder and cook for a further 1 minute.
3 Stir in the rice and add 450ml (¾pt) of the haddock cooking water. When it comes up to simmering point, cover with the lid and cook very gently on the simmering plate for 15–20 minutes or until the rice grains are tender.
4 Flake the fish and add to the rice with the hard-boiled eggs, parsley, lemon juice and seasoning. Serve immediately.

450g (1lb) smoked haddock fillets
50g (2oz) butter
1 onion, chopped
1×5ml sp (1tsp) curry powder
225g (8oz) brown long-grain rice
3 hard-boiled eggs, chopped
3×15ml sp (3tbsp) fresh chopped parsley
1×15ml sp (1tbsp) lemon juice
salt and pepper

Note: Although this dish was traditionally served for breakfast it also makes a good lunch or supper dish served with a salad.

25g (1oz) all-bran
4×15ml sp (4tbsp) milk
225g (8oz) wholemeal self-raising
  flour
1×2.5ml sp (½tsp) salt
25g (1oz) butter
1 egg
milk for brushing

Good Morning Scones

1 Stir together the all-bran and milk and leave for about 10 minutes until all the liquid has been absorbed.
2 Stir together the flour and salt and rub in the butter until the mixture resembles fine breadcrumbs.
3 Beat the egg into the soaked bran mixture, pour it onto the flour and stir quickly to form a dough. Knead lightly and shape into an 18cm (7in) round. Brush with a little milk and place on a greased baking tray.
4 Bake at 425°F (220°C) or at the top of the roasting oven for 10–12 minutes. Serve warm with cottage cheese and raisins, or Scrambled Eggs.

225g (8oz) dried pears
225g (8oz) prunes
110g (4oz) dried peaches
110g (4oz) dried apple rings
1 cinnamon stick
8 cloves
300ml (½pt) water
300ml (½pt) apple juice
50g (2oz) walnut pieces
50g (2oz) whole almonds

Spiced Fruit Compote

1 Place the fruits, cinnamon stick, cloves, water and apple juice in a large casserole and cook at 350°F (180°C) or in the centre of the roasting oven for 20 minutes. Place in the simmering oven for 2–3 hours.
2 Remove the cinnamon stick and add the nuts mixing carefully so as not to damage the fruit.
3 Serve hot or cold with yoghurt, whipped cream or fromage frais as a dessert or with muesli or oatmeal biscuits for breakfast.

Note: It is best to choose 'no-soak' fruits, but if these are not available soak the fruits in the apple juice and water for about 8 hours.

1.5kg (3lb) tangerines
6 lemons
2.5 litre (5pt) water
1.5kg (3lb) sugar

Tangerine Marmalade *colour opposite*

1 Scrub all the fruit, then dry it.
2 Cut the tangerines in half and squeeze out all the juice. Remove the membranes including pips with a teaspoon and cut the peel into narrow strips (tangerines do not have any pith). Peel the lemons and slice thinly, discarding pips.
3 Put juice, peel and water into a large saucepan or preserving pan and bring to the boil on the boiling plate. Simmer very gently on the simmering plate without covering until the peel is absolutely tender (you should be able to squeeze it apart with your thumb and forefinger); this will take about 30 minutes.
4 Stir in the sugar and let it dissolve, then boil the marmalade for approximately 30 minutes or until setting point is reached.
5 Remove the pan from the heat and let it settle for 15 minutes. As soon as the marmalade has cooled enough and the fruit has stopped floating on the surface and is evenly distributed throughout the liquid, pour into warmed jars and cover with a waxed disc. Seal and label when cold.

Note: Tangerines are not always available but any similar fruit, eg mineolas, will do just as well.

Tangerine Marmalade (Kenwood)

1 × 15ml sp (1tbsp) sunflower
  seeds
2 × 15ml sp (2tbsp) apple juice
225g (8oz) white cabbage
110g (4oz) celery
2 dessert apples
2 × 15ml sp (2tbsp) sunflower oil
1 × 15ml sp (1tbsp) white wine
  vinegar
1 × 5ml sp (1tsp) fresh chopped
  tarragon

Apple, Celery and Sunflower Seed Salad

1   Soak the sunflower seeds in the apple juice for about 30 minutes so that they swell up.
2   Finely shred the cabbage and celery. Wash the apples and cut into quarters, slice thinly.
3   In a large bowl mix together the sunflower oil, vinegar and tarragon. Add the cabbage, celery and apples and toss so that they become well coated. Finally, stir in the soaked sunflower seeds, reserving a few to sprinkle on top.
4   Transfer the salad to a serving dish and sprinkle on the remaining sunflower seeds.

225g (8oz) rhubarb
225g (8oz) red currants
225g (8oz) blackcurrants
75g (3oz) soft brown sugar
110g (4oz) raspberries
110g (4oz) strawberries
3 × 15ml sp (3tbsp) cherry brandy
8 slices brown bread, crusts
  removed

Summer Pudding   *colour opposite*

1   Place the rhubarb, currants and sugar in a heavy pan and cook gently on the simmering plate for 10–15 minutes until tender. Add the raspberries, strawberries and cherry brandy and leave to cool. Strain the fruit, reserving the juice.
2   Cut 3 circles of bread the same increasing diameter as a 900ml (1½pt) pudding basin. Shape the remaining bread to fit round the sides of the basin. Soak all the bread in the reserved juice.
3   Line the bottom of the basin with one of the circles then arrange the shaped bread round the sides. Pour in half the fruit and place another circle on top. Cover with the remaining fruit and over this place the third circle of bread.
4   Cover with a plate or saucer to fit inside the basin and put a small weight on top. Leave in the refrigerator overnight.
5   Turn onto a serving dish and pour over any remaining fruit juice. Serve with whipped cream or fromage frais.

Variation for individual Summer Puddings:
1   As stage 1 above.
2   Cut out 8 × 7.5cm (3in) circles of bread; cut remaining bread into 2.5cm (1in) wide strips. Soak all the bread in the reserved juice.
3   Line the bases of 4 ramekin dishes with circles of bread and arrange the strips to fit the sides. Divide the fruit between the dishes and top with the remaining circles.
4   Cover each dish with greaseproof paper and stand one on top of the other on saucers, with a saucer carrying a small weight on top. Leave overnight in the refrigerator.
5   Turn onto individual dishes and serve any remaining fruit separately.

*Individual Summer Puddings
(John West Foods Ltd)*

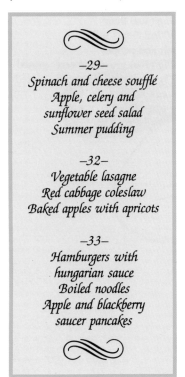

–29–
*Spinach and cheese soufflé
Apple, celery and
sunflower seed salad
Summer pudding*

–32–
*Vegetable lasagne
Red cabbage coleslaw
Baked apples with apricots*

–33–
*Hamburgers with
hungarian sauce
Boiled noodles
Apple and blackberry
saucer pancakes*

8 strips lasagne (preferably
   wholewheat)
450g (1lb) calabrese
1 onion, finely chopped
2×15ml sp (2tbsp) oil
1 clove garlic, crushed
3×5ml sp (3tsp) dried oregano
1×400g (14oz) can tomatoes,
   chopped with their juices
salt and pepper
Sauce:
175g (6oz) button mushrooms,
   sliced
25g (1oz) butter
25g (1oz) flour
300ml (½pt) milk
75g (3oz) cheddar cheese

Vegetable Lasagne

1   If the pasta requires pre-cooking, boil in plenty of boiling water and
    a little oil, to help keep it apart, for 8–10 minutes. Drain and rinse in
    cold water.
2   Cook the calabrese gently in a little boiling water until just tender,
    drain.
3   Gently fry the onion in the oil on the simmering plate for a few
    minutes, then add garlic, oregano, canned tomatoes and seasoning.
    Cover the pan and cook for a further 10 minutes so that the flavours
    can blend.
4   Now prepare the sauce. Sauté the sliced mushrooms in the butter,
    then add the flour and cook gently for 1 minute. Gradually stir in
    the milk and continue to cook on the simmering plate until the sauce
    is thickened and smooth.
5   Place half the calabrese in a square or rectangular 1.75 litre (3pt)
    ovenproof dish. Spoon over some of the tomato mixture, cover with 2
    or 3 pieces of lasagne and then a coating of sauce. Repeat these layers
    ending with the mushroom sauce. Sprinkle over the grated cheese and
    bake at 400°F (200°C) or in the centre of the roasting oven for 25–30
    minutes until the cheese is bubbling and golden. Serve immediately.

225g (8oz) red cabbage
110g (4oz) black grapes
8 radishes
110g (4oz) walnuts

Vinaigrette dressing:
1×15ml sp (1tbsp) red wine
   vinegar
3×15ml sp (3tbsp) sunflower oil
pinch mustard powder
pinch paprika

Red Cabbage Coleslaw

1   Wash and finely shred the cabbage removing any tough outside leaves
    and the core.
2   Wash the grapes, slice in half and remove the pips.
3   Wash and slice the radishes and roughly chop the walnuts.
4   Mix these ingredients with the red cabbage.
5   Mix together the vinaigrette ingredients in a screw-top jar and shake
    thoroughly. Toss the salad in the dressing.
6   Place in a large serving bowl and serve immediately.

4 large cooking apples
50g (2oz) no-soak dried apricots,
   chopped
25g (1oz) raisins
25g (1oz) soft brown sugar
1×2.5ml sp (½tsp) ground
   cloves
4×15ml sp (4tbsp) cider

Baked Apples with Apricots

1   Remove the cores from the apples and make a shallow cut round the
    middle of each.
2   Mix together the apricots, raisins, sugar and cloves and use to fill the
    apple cavities, pressing down firmly.
3   Place in an ovenproof dish and add the cider. Bake at 350°F (180°C)
    or in the centre of the roasting oven for 50–60 minutes or until soft.
4   Serve hot with cream or custard.

Variation (colour page 59):
Mix together 50g (2oz) roughly chopped walnuts with 25g (1oz) sultanas
and 1×2.5ml sp (½tsp) ground cloves. Fill the apple cavities, pressing
down firmly, and then drizzle 1×15ml sp (1tbsp) honey mixed with
2×15ml sp (2tbsp) water over the top in place of the cider.

Hamburgers with Hungarian Sauce

1 Mix the minced meat, salt and pepper and chopped onion together. Divide into 4 and shape into round flat hamburgers.
2 Place in a shallow heatproof dish in the meat tin hung on the top set of runners in the roasting oven and grill for 10 minutes on each side. Alternatively, the hamburgers may be pan fried in a little vegetable oil. Remove and keep hot in the simmering oven.
3 Fry the sliced onion in the vegetable oil until soft. Add the sliced mushrooms. When cooked remove from the pan and keep hot.
4 Stir into the pan juices the flour, paprika, chopped tomatoes, tomato purée, lemon juice, stock and seasoning. Keep stirring on the simmering plate until the sauce thickens. Return onions and mushrooms to the pan then pour over the hamburgers.
5 Drizzle over the soured cream and serve immediately, accompanied by boiled noodles.

340g (12oz) lean minced beef
salt and pepper
75g (3oz) onions, finely chopped
225g (8oz) onions, sliced
2×15ml sp (2tbsp) vegetable oil
110g (4oz) button mushrooms, sliced
25g (1oz) flour
2×15ml sp (2tbsp) paprika
1×200g (7oz) can tomatoes with their juices
2×15ml sp (2tbsp) tomato purée
1×15ml sp (1tbsp) lemon juice
300ml (½pt) chicken stock
salt and pepper
4×15ml sp (4tbsp) soured cream

Apple and Blackberry Saucer Pancakes

1   Mix together the flour and sugar, then beat in the egg yolk and milk and continue to beat to a smooth batter. Whisk the egg white until stiff and fold in.
2   Butter 6 large saucers and place on baking sheets. Divide the batter between them.
3   Bake at 425°F (220°C) or at the top of the roasting oven for 15–20 minutes until set and golden.
4   Meanwhile peel, core and slice the apples and cook with the blackberries until soft.
5   When they are cooked, slide the pancakes off the saucers, hollow side up, onto a warmed serving dish and fill with the hot fruit mixture. Serve immediately.

Note: This method of cooking pancakes is simple to do and cuts out any unpleasant frying smells. Serve them with any fresh fruit or homemade jam.

Piperade

1 Heat the oil in a large frying pan and fry the onions and peppers gently until softened.
2 Add the garlic, tomatoes and seasoning and simmer for 5 minutes.
3 Beat the eggs with the milk and pour onto the cooked vegetables. Keeping the pan on the simmering plate, cook gently for 3–4 minutes, stirring occasionally until the eggs are set.
4 Spoon onto a hot dish and serve immediately with toast. Alternatively, place the bacon rashers in the roasting tin hung on the top set of runners, and grill until cooked. Place on top of the piperade and serve immediately.

2 × 15ml sp (2tbsp) vegetable oil
1 large onion, sliced
1 red pepper, cored, seeded and sliced
1 green pepper, cored, seeded and sliced
2 cloves garlic, crushed
225g (8oz) tomatoes, skinned and chopped
salt and pepper
6 eggs
2 × 15ml sp (2tbsp) milk

to serve: triangles of fresh toast
6 rashers of streaky bacon, rinded

Toffeed Rice Pudding

1 Place the milk, half the sugar, butter, rice and vanilla essence in a saucepan on the simmering plate and bring gently to the boil.
2 Transfer to an ovenproof dish and place in the simmering oven for 2–3 hours, or bake at 300°F (150°C) for 2 hours.
3 Cool the rice slightly, then stir in the cream and the mixed peel. Chill well.
4 Spread the remaining sugar over the rice. Place in the meat tin and hang on the top set of runners in the roasting oven until the sugar has caramelised to a golden brown. Allow to cool slightly before serving.

600ml (1pt) milk
110g (4oz) caster sugar
25g (1oz) butter
50g (2oz) pudding rice
1 × 5ml sp (1tsp) vanilla essence
4 × 15ml sp (4tbsp) single cream
50g (2oz) candied peel

Spaghetti Provençale

1 Heat the oil in a large pan or cast iron casserole and fry the onions and garlic gently on the simmering plate for a few minutes.
2 Add the prepared vegetables to the pan and fry for a few more minutes.
3 Add the tomato purée, herbs, seasoning and stock and simmer gently for a further 20 minutes with the pan covered. Alternatively, place in the centre of the baking oven for 20 minutes or in the simmering oven for 1 hour.
4 Meanwhile, cook the spaghetti in plenty of boiling salted water for 10–12 minutes or until just tender.
5 Drain and put into a gratin dish, top with the sauce and serve immediately.
6 For a more substantial dish sprinkle over the breadcrumbs and cheese and brown at the top of the roasting oven.

2 × 15ml sp (2tbsp) vegetable oil
1 onion, peeled and chopped
1 clove garlic, crushed
450g (1lb) courgettes, washed and sliced
340g (12oz) mushrooms, sliced
1 red pepper, cored, seeded and diced
1 yellow pepper, cored, seeded and diced
3 × 15ml sp (3tbsp) tomato purée
1 × 5ml sp (1tsp) dried basil
1 × 5ml sp (1tsp) dried marjoram
salt and pepper
600ml (1pt) vegetable or chicken stock
340g (12oz) wholewheat spaghetti
50g (2oz) brown breadcrumbs (optional)
50g (2oz) grated cheese (optional)

75g (3oz) butter
175g (6oz) plain flour
25g (1oz) sugar
2 egg yolks
900g (2lb) cooking apples
25g (1oz) butter
50g (2oz) caster sugar
1×15ml sp (1tbsp) water
juice of ½ lemon
3×15ml sp (3tbsp) apricot jam to
   glaze

French Apple Flan *colour page 115*

1   Rub the butter into the flour, stir in the sugar and add the egg yolks, mixing to a dough. Use to line a 18cm (7in) loose-bottomed metal flan tin, prick and leave to rest.
2   Peel and slice the apples. Reserve one to decorate the top and cook the remainder with the butter, sugar and water. Purée, add the lemon juice, cool.
3   When cold, pour the apple purée into the pastry case and arrange the remaining apple, thinly sliced, in circles on the top.
4   Bake at 400°F (200°C) or in the centre of the roasting oven for 35–40 minutes.
5   Meanwhile make the glaze by heating the apricot jam with 1×5ml sp (1tsp) water and then sieving.
6   Glaze the flan as soon as it is cooked and allow to cool in the tin.

110g (4oz) wholemeal flour
pinch of salt
4×15ml sp (4tbsp) water
25g (1oz) lard

Filling:
110g (4oz) bacon, finely chopped
40g (1½oz) butter
40g (1½oz) flour
150ml (¼pt) milk
75g (3oz) mature cheddar cheese
1×15ml sp (1tbsp) wholegrain
   mustard
salt and pepper
275g (10oz) curd cheese or sieved
   cottage cheese
3 eggs, separated
4×15ml sp (4tbsp) soured cream
   or crème fraîche

Topping:
2 tomatoes, sliced
50g (2oz) cheddar cheese, grated

Cheese and Bacon Cheesecake

1   Sift the flour and salt into a bowl. Put the water and lard into a pan over gentle heat and stir until the fat has melted. Pour onto the flour and mix to a soft smooth dough.
2   While still warm, press evenly over the base of a greased loose-bottomed 18–20cm (7–8in) round cake tin, working the dough up the sides of the tin to a depth of about 2.5cm (1in). It will be fairly thin.
3   To make the filling, fry the bacon in its own fat over a low heat for about 5 minutes or until cooked. Remove from the pan with a slotted spoon and keep to one side.
4   Put the butter, flour and milk into a pan and cook over a gentle heat, whisking all the time until smooth and thickened, cook for a further minute. Remove from heat and stir in the cheese, mustard and seasoning.
5   Soften the curd cheese in a large mixing bowl. Beat in the cheese sauce, egg yolks and soured cream or crème fraîche.
6   Whisk the egg whites until stiff and fold lightly but thoroughly into the cheese mixture together with the bacon. Spoon the mixture into the prepared tin and bake at 325°F (160°C) in the baking oven or on the grid shelf at the bottom of the roasting oven protected by the solid shelf, for 1½ hours. If necessary, once set, transfer the cheesecake to the simmering oven for the remainder of the cooking time.
7   Arrange the tomato slices on top of the cheesecake and sprinkle with the grated cheese. Return to the oven for a further 10–15 minutes.
8   Ease the sides of the tin carefully away from the cheesecake and lift the hot cooked cheesecake out on the tin base. Serve immediately.

Leek and Courgette Salad

1 Slice the leeks and courgettes very thinly — use a food processor if you have one.
2 Place the hazelnuts on a baking sheet and roast at 350°F (180°C) or in the centre of the roasting oven for 8–10 minutes. Allow to cool, then chop.
3 Blend the tomatoes, tomato purée and lemon juice, then add the oil, oregano and garlic and mix well.
4 Place the leeks, courgettes and hazelnuts in a large salad bowl, pour over the dressing and toss.

2 large leeks
450g (1lb) courgettes
50g (2oz) hazelnuts
2 tomatoes, skinned and chopped
1×15ml sp (1tbsp) tomato purée
juice of ½ lemon
1×15ml sp (1tbsp) vegetable oil
1×2.5ml sp (½tsp) oregano
1 clove garlic, crushed

Pear Syllabub

1 Soak the pears overnight in the wine, then cook gently in a covered pan for 20 minutes or until soft. Alternatively, place the pears in the wine in an ovenproof dish in the bottom oven overnight. Add extra fruit juice or water if necessary to stop them drying up. Leave to cool.
2 Liquidise or sieve the pears with some of the cooking liquid to obtain a smooth purée.
3 Whisk the egg whites until stiff then whisk in the sugar.
4 Fold in the fruit purée and whipped cream.
5 Pile the mixture into glasses or small dishes and chill for 3–4 hours. Decorate with chopped nuts.

110g (4oz) dried pears
150ml (¼pt) white wine
2 egg whites
25g (1oz) soft brown sugar
150ml (¼pt) double cream, whipped
chopped nuts to decorate

Variation:
Any dried fruit may be used for this dessert such as peaches, apricots or prunes.

Wholemeal Pizza

1 Grease a circular pizza tray 28cm (11in) in diameter.
2 Combine the flour, salt and sesame seeds in a bowl. Then whisk the yeast and sugar into the warm water. Leave it to get a frothy head (about 10 minutes in a warm place).
3 Stir the frothed yeast mixture into the dry ingredients and mix to a smooth dough. Knead on a flat surface for 5 minutes.
4 Roll out the dough into a circle the size of the pizza tray. Place it on the greased tin and stretch it if necessary to the edge. Slide the tin into a greased plastic bag and leave the dough to rise in a warm place while the topping is prepared.
5 Heat the oil and gently fry the onion, celery and garlic for 5 minutes, then add the pepper and mushrooms and cook for a further 3 minutes. Stir in half the basil, the chopped tomatoes and the tomato purée and

225g (8oz) wholemeal flour
1×2.5ml sp (½tsp) salt
1×15ml sp (1tbsp) sesame seeds
1×5ml sp (1tsp) dried yeast
1×5ml sp (1tsp) sugar
170ml (6fl oz) hand-hot water

Topping:
2×15ml sp (2tbsp) sunflower oil
1 onion, chopped
2 sticks celery, sliced
1 clove garlic, crushed
1 green pepper, cored, seeded and sliced
50g (2oz) button mushrooms, sliced (cont)

2×15ml sp (2tbsp) fresh chopped
  basil or
1×5ml sp (1tsp) dried basil
1×400g (14oz) can Italian
  tomatoes, chopped with their
  juices
1×15ml sp (1tbsp) tomato purée
salt and pepper
110g (4oz) mozzarella cheese, cut
  into small pieces
25g (1oz) pumpkin or sunflower
  seeds (optional)

½ small head of cauliflower, cut
  into florets
225g (8oz) broccoli
1 yellow pepper, cored, seeded
  and sliced
1 red pepper, cored, seeded and
  sliced

Dressing:
1×15ml sp (1tbsp) sunflower oil
1×15ml sp (1tbsp) white wine
  vinegar
1×15ml sp (1tbsp) apple juice
2×5ml sp (2tsp) fresh tarragon

1 pink grapefruit
1 ordinary grapefruit
2 oranges
4 clementines
150g (5oz) quark or curd cheese
1×150ml (5fl oz) tub greek
  yoghurt
110g (4oz) muscovado sugar
25g (1oz) flaked almonds

*Citrus Fruit Brulée (Dairy
Produce Advisory Service, Milk
Marketing Board)*

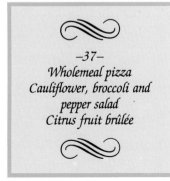

–37–
*Wholemeal pizza
Cauliflower, broccoli and
pepper salad
Citrus fruit brûlée*

season. Simmer the sauce for 15 minutes or until reduced to a thick
jam-like consistency.

6 Remove the pizza from the bag and spread the tomato mixture over the
top nearly to the edge. Lay the pieces of cheese on the top and scatter
over the remaining basil and the pumpkin or sunflower seeds.

7 Bake at 425°F (220°C) or near the top of the roasting oven, for 20–30
minutes. Serve piping hot.

Variations:
There are many variations for toppings including olives, anchovies, capers,
salami, ham, tuna, sardines – anything and everything can be used.

Cauliflower, Broccoli and Pepper Salad

1 Par-boil the cauliflower florets and the broccoli until cooked but still
crunchy. Drain and cool.

2 Place the cauliflower and broccoli in a large bowl with the yellow and
red peppers.

3 Mix together the dressing ingredients, pour over the salad and toss
gently to coat.

Citrus Fruit Brûlée *colour opposite*

1 First prepare the fruit by peeling the grapefruit then paring the skin
from each segment. Peel the oranges, removing all pith and membrane,
then slice across into rounds. Peel the clementines and segment.

2 Place all the fruit in a flameproof shallow serving dish, spreading it out
as evenly as possible.

3 Now mix together the cheese and the yoghurt and spread evenly over
the fruit.

4 Crumble up the muscovado sugar, mix with the flaked almonds and
sprinkle thickly over the surface.

5 Place the dish in a meat tin hung on the top set of runners in the
roasting oven and grill until the sugar begins to melt and bubble. Do
not take your eyes off it for one moment. Then remove it from the oven,
cool, and chill in the refrigerator until needed. The sugar should harden
into a golden crust which cracks as you put the spoon in, revealing the
soft creamy mixture and fruit beneath.

Variations:
You can use any fruit you have to hand for a brûlée, eg mixed summer fruits
such as raspberries, red and black currants, loganberries and strawberries;
bananas, grapes, tinned pineapples; or even chopped dried fruits such as
apricots, peaches, apples and nuts.

4 large baking potatoes
oil for brushing
butter to serve

Dinner Jackets

1   Scrub the potatoes thoroughly and dry. Brush all over with oil and bake at 400°F (200°C) or in a roasting tin in the centre of the roasting oven for 1–1½ hours or until soft.
2   Cut a deep cross in the top of each potato, fill with butter and serve immediately, or use any of the following fillings.

Stilton and Bacon

4 rashers streaky bacon, derinded
  and diced
110g (4oz) stilton cheese,
  crumbled
fresh chives, chopped

1   Lightly fry the bacon in a pan until crisp. Divide between the potatoes and crumble the stilton cheese onto the top. Sprinkle on a few chopped chives and serve immediately.

Prawn and Tuna

110g (4oz) cooked peeled prawns
1×185g (7oz) can tuna, drained
  and flaked
4×15ml sp (4tbsp) greek yoghurt
  or soured cream
1×15ml sp (1tsp) creamed
  horseradish
salt and pepper

1   Mix all the ingredients together and season to taste.
2   Spoon into the hot split potatoes.

Other suggestions for fillings:
Chopped cooked chipolatas with a sauce made with passatta, chopped spring onions, wholegrain mustard and seasoning.
Sliced raw mushrooms with a curry sauce made with soured cream, mango chutney, mayonnaise, curry powder and seasoning, garnished with chopped parsley.

Strawberry and Almond Swirl

1 Lightly crush the strawberries, reserving a few for decoration, and place in a bowl. Stir in the sugar. Gently fold in half the yoghurt.
2 Place remaining yoghurt in another bowl and fold in the chopped nuts.
3 Spoon half the strawberry mixture into the bottom of 4 individual glass dishes. Spoon over three-quarters of the almond mixture and top with the remaining strawberry mixture. Swirl gently with a skewer or cocktail stick.
4 Spoon over the remaining almond mixture and swirl again.
5 Top with the whole strawberries and chill until required.

225g (8oz) fresh or frozen strawberries
25g (1oz) caster sugar
1×450g (16oz) carton greek yoghurt
50g (2oz) almonds, roughly chopped

Chilli Beef Stuffed Tacos with Salad

1 Gently fry the onion and garlic in the vegetable oil until soft.
2 Add the minced beef and fry rapidly to seal.
3 Add the chilli powder, oregano and ground cumin and fry for a further 2 minutes.
4 Stir in the flour, tomato purée and canned tomatoes, followed by the beef stock; season. Either continue to cook on the simmering plate for 1 hour or cook in the simmering oven for 2–3 hours at 300°F (150°C).
5 Warm the taco shells in the simmering oven. Carefully fill with the chilli beef mixture and place flat side down in an ovenproof dish. Sprinkle the cheese over the top and grill in the roasting oven for about 5 minutes or until the cheese is melted but not browned.
6 Remove from the oven and place two tacos on each plate. Top with the shredded lettuce, tomatoes, cucumber and avocado. Serve at once.

1 large onion, diced
1 clove garlic, crushed
1×15ml sp (1tbsp) vegetable oil
450g (1lb) lean minced beef
1×15ml sp (1tbsp) chilli powder
1×2.5ml sp (½tsp) oregano
1×2.5ml sp (½tsp) ground cumin
25g (1oz) flour
1×15ml sp (1tbsp) tomato purée
1×400g (14oz) can tomatoes, chopped with their juices
300ml (½pt) beef stock
salt and pepper
8 taco shells
110g (4oz) cheddar cheese
½ iceberg lettuce, shredded
4 tomatoes, sliced
½ cucumber, chopped
1 avocado, peeled and sliced

Orange Crème Caramel

1 Put the granulated sugar, water and orange juice in a pan and heat gently on the simmering plate until dissolved, then cook to a rich caramel without stirring. Pour the caramel into a 900ml (1½pt) soufflé dish and leave to set.
2 Beat together the eggs, egg yolk and caster sugar.
3 Heat the milk almost to boiling point and add to the eggs, mix well and strain through a sieve; stir in the orange rind.
4 Pour into the soufflé dish and place in a roasting tin containing sufficient water to come halfway up the sides of the dish. Make sure the water is boiling. Cover the soufflé dish with greaseproof paper and then foil.
5 Bake at 300°F (150°C) for 1½ hours until set, or hang on the lowest set of runners in the roasting oven for 15 minutes then transfer to the

75g (3oz) granulated sugar
1×15ml sp (1tbsp) water
juice of 1 orange
3 eggs
1 egg yolk
25g (1oz) caster sugar
450ml (¾pt) milk
grated rind of 1 orange

-40-
Dinner jackets
Strawberry and almond swirl

-41-
Chilli beef stuffed tacos
with salad
Orange crème caramel

-42-
Fish chowder
Herby french bread
French lemon tart

-45-
Buck rarebit
Golden greengage bake

simmering oven for 1½ hours. For the 4-oven Aga, hang on the middle set of runners in the baking oven for 15 minutes then transfer to the simmering oven for 1½ hours. Leave until cold, then refrigerate until required.

6   Unmould onto a flat serving dish.

Notes: This dish may be served with segmented oranges.

To check if a baked custard is cooked, make a small incision in the top with the point of a knife. The knife should come out clean. After cooking always remove the custard from the water bath and leave until completely cold, preferably chilled, before unmoulding.

Variations:
Vanilla: add 1×5ml sp (1tsp) vanilla essence to the custard.
Chocolate: add 75g (3oz) dark bitter chocolate to the milk and melt completely.

175g (6oz) streaky bacon, rinded
1 onion, sliced
2 sticks celery, sliced
2 medium sized potatoes, diced
600ml (1pt) water
salt and pepper
1×15ml sp (1tbsp) flour
600ml (1pt) milk
225g (8oz) frozen sweetcorn
  kernels or 1 small can sweetcorn
340g (12oz) smoked haddock,
  skinned and cubed,
or 1×198g (7oz) can tuna chunks
  in brine,
or 1×213g (8½oz) can pink
  salmon,
or 1×400g (14oz) can baby clams
fresh chopped parsley to garnish

Fish Chowder *colour opposite*

1   Gently fry bacon in a large pan until the fat runs, add the onion and celery and cook for 2 minutes. Then add the potato, water and seasoning and cook gently until the potato is tender (about 15 minutes). Remove from heat.

2   Mix the flour with a little milk and stir it into the soup. Add the remaining milk, the sweetcorn and fish and bring to the boil. Simmer gently for 10–15 minutes or until the fish is cooked. Alternatively, bring the chowder to the boil, then place in the simmering oven for 1 hour. Serve hot sprinkled with a little freshly chopped parsley.

1 french stick, granary or white
2×15ml sp (2tbsp) chopped fresh
  herbs, choose whatever is
  available but dill goes well with
  fish as do parsley, thyme and
  tarragon
110g (4oz) butter

Herby French Bread

1   Slice the bread neatly across at an angle of 45 degrees making the slices about 2cm (¾in) thick. Cutting at an angle means that the herbs and butter soak into the bread rather then run out between the slices.

2   Mix together the herbs and butter and carefully spread on the partially sliced bread – any herby butter remaining can be spread on the top.

3   Wrap in foil and bake at 400°F (200°C) or in the centre of the roasting oven for 20 minutes.

4   Open up the foil and cook for a further 10 minutes uncovered to crisp the top. Serve immediately.

Fish Chowder (John West Foods Ltd)

75g (3oz) butter
175g (6oz) plain flour
25g (1oz) caster sugar
2 egg yolks
110g (4oz) caster sugar
1 egg
1 lemon, juice and rind
50g (2oz) softened butter

French Lemon Tart

1 Rub the butter into the flour until it resembles breadcrumbs. Stir in the 25g (1oz) sugar and egg yolks and work lightly to a dough, adding a little water if necessary to bring it together. Cool for 30 minutes.

2 Roll out pastry and line a 15cm (6in) loose-bottomed flan tin; prick with a fork. Line with a circle of greaseproof paper filled with baking beans and bake blind at 425°F (220°C) or at the top of the roasting oven for 10 minutes. Remove baking beans and greaseproof paper.

3 Beat together the 110g (4oz) caster sugar and egg until light and creamy, add lemon juice, grated rind and softened butter and mix well to a smooth paste.

4 Pour filling into the partially cooked pastry case and bake at 350°F (180°C) at the bottom of the roasting oven on the grid shelf or in the baking oven, for 10–15 minutes. Serve warm or cold – this tart will keep for several days.

Buck Rarebit

1 Place the cheese, butter, mustard, seasoning and beer in a pan and heat gently on the simmering plate until a creamy mixture is obtained.
2 Meanwhile poach the eggs and toast the bread.
3 Pour the cheese mixture over the toast and grill near the top of the roasting oven until golden and bubbling, then top each slice with a poached egg and serve immediately.

225g (8oz) cheddar cheese, grated
25g (1oz) butter
1×5ml sp (1tsp) wholegrain mustard
salt and pepper
4×15ml sp (4tbsp) beer
4 eggs
4 slices wholemeal bread

Golden Greengage Bake

1 Place 75g (3oz) of the oatmeal on a baking tray and toast at the top of the roasting oven; cool. Quarter the fruit and mix with 25g (1oz) of the toasted oatmeal. Place three-quarters of this mixture in a 2 litre (4pt) shallow ovenproof dish.
2 Split cardamom pods and remove seeds; crush using a pestle and mortar or rolling pin.
3 Beat together the butter and sugar and the cardamom seeds. Gradually beat in the quark and soured cream or yoghurt, egg yolks and remaining toasted oatmeal.
4 Whisk egg whites and fold into the cheese mixture. Spoon over the greengages and scatter the remaining fruit mixture over; sprinkle over the remaining oatmeal.
5 Stand dish on a baking sheet and bake at 350°F (180°C) or near the bottom of the roasting oven for about 50 minutes or until just set and golden brown. Cool for about 15 minutes before serving.

Variations:
The greengages may be replaced by damsons or plums if preferred.

110g (4oz) medium oatmeal
1kg (2lb) greengages
3 green cardamoms
75g (3oz) butter
75g (3oz) soft brown sugar
1×225g (8oz) carton quark
1×150ml (5fl oz) tub soured cream or greek yoghurt
2 eggs, separated

Ham and Cheese Ring

1 In a bowl mix together the crumbled cheese, cooked ham, onion and pickle, blending well together.
2 Roll out pastry on a lightly floured surface to a rectangle measuring 40×28cm (16×11in).
3 Spread the cheese filling over the pastry to within 1cm (½in) of the edges. Brush the edges with beaten egg and roll up like a Swiss roll from one of the long edges, press firmly to seal.
4 Using scissors, snip across the long edge of the roll at 2.5cm (1in) intervals, almost through to the other edge.
5 Shape the roll into a ring, brush the ends with beaten egg and press together to seal firmly. (cont)

175g (6oz) stilton cheese, crumbled
110g (4oz) cooked ham, sliced thinly
1 onion, finely chopped
2×15ml sp (2tbsp) mild pickle or homemade chutney
1×398g (13oz) packet frozen puff pastry, thawed
beaten egg to glaze
poppy seeds or sesame seeds

Bramble Fool (Dairy Produce Advisory Service, Milk Marketing Board)

6   Carefully lift each section of the ring and tilt to expose the filling. Brush the ring with beaten egg and sprinkle with poppy seeds or sesame seeds.
7   Bake at 400°F (200°C) or near the top of the roasting oven for 30–35 minutes or until golden brown and cooked through. Allow to cool slightly and serve warm.

Mangetout Salad

250g (8oz) mangetout
110g (4oz) button mushrooms
1 red pepper, cored, seeded and sliced
1 × 15ml sp (1tbsp) sesame seeds, toasted
3 × 15ml sp (3tbsp) sunflower oil
1 × 15ml sp (1tbsp) white wine vinegar
1 × 5ml sp (1tsp) french mustard
1 clove garlic, crushed
salt and pepper

1   Top and tail the mangetout and blanch in boiling water for 2 minutes. Drain and cool.
2   Trim the mushroom stalks level with the caps. Wipe with a damp cloth and place in a bowl with the red pepper, cooled mangetout and sesame seeds.
3   Place all the remaining ingredients in a screw-top jar and shake to blend. Pour over the salad and toss thoroughly.

Bramble Fool *colour opposite*

225g (8oz) blackberries
1 × 15ml sp (1tbsp) water
75g (3oz) sugar
1 egg white
1 × 150ml (5fl oz) carton double or whipping cream, whipped until stiff

1   Simmer the blackberries in the water for about 10 minutes until soft. Leave to cool, set 4 aside for decoration, then purée and sieve to remove seeds. Stir in 50g (2oz) of the sugar and chill until very cold.
2   Whisk the egg white until stiff, then whisk in the remaining sugar until glossy; fold in the whipped cream. Reserve a little for decoration.
3   Fold the blackberry purée into the cream mixture and spoon into individual glasses. Top with reserved cream mixture and blackberries. Chill until required. If preferred spoon a few stewed blackberries into the bottom of the glasses before adding the fool.

Variations:
Use this recipe as a basic guide for almost any type of fruit fool. Follow as above for fruits which are normally cooked before serving. Other soft fruits such as raspberries and strawberries simply need puréeing and sieving to remove any seeds. You will need about 150ml (¼pt) prepared purée, sweetened to taste.

–45–
Ham and cheese ring
Mangetout salad
Bramble fool

–48–
Spinach roulade
Red, white and green salad
Strawberry cheese tartlets

–49–
Smoked haddock gougère
Tomato salad
Apple and raspberry torte

450g (1lb) spinach
4 eggs, separated
pinch of nutmeg
salt and pepper

Filling:
2 × 15ml sp (2tbsp) vegetable oil
1 small onion, chopped
175g (6oz) button mushrooms,
  sliced
25g (1oz) flour
300ml (½pt) milk
150g (5oz) mature cheddar
  cheese, grated
salt and pepper

Spinach Roulade

1   Line the base of a 30 × 20 cm (12 × 8in) Swiss roll tin with lightly greased greaseproof paper.
2   Cook the spinach in a large pan, with just the water clinging to the leaves after washing, for 6–8 minutes. Drain well and chop finely.
3   Mix the egg yolks with the cooked spinach and season with the nutmeg, salt and pepper. Whisk the egg whites until moist and forming soft peaks and carefully fold into the spinach mixture.
4   Spread the mixture evenly in the prepared tin and cook at 400°F (200°C) or in the centre of the roasting oven for 10–15 minutes, until risen and firm.
5   Heat the oil in a pan, add the onion and fry until soft; add the mushrooms and cook for a further 2 minutes. Stir in the flour, then gradually add the milk, stirring constantly, until the sauce has boiled. Remove from the pan and stir in 110g (4oz) of the cheese; season to taste.
6   When the roulade is cooked, remove from the oven, turn out onto a clean sheet of greaseproof or silicon paper and peel off the lining paper. Spread some of the sauce over the roulade and roll up like a Swiss roll using the paper to ease it into shape. Don't try to roll it too tightly and do expect it to crack slightly.
7   Ease onto a baking sheet or ovenproof dish and pour over the remaining sauce. Sprinkle with the remaining cheese and pop back into the oven at the same temperature for 5 minutes until the cheese has browned. Serve immediately.

Note: A roulade is basically a soufflé cooked on a tray the size of a Swiss roll tin and then rolled up with a filling. Most savoury roulades are made using 300ml (½pt) of white sauce to which has been added 3 egg yolks and 3 whisked egg whites plus a suitable flavouring, eg 75g (3oz) grated cheese, ham, cooked smoked haddock. Roulades can be filled with a flavoured sauce and served hot or rolled up and allowed to cool and then filled with a flavoured mayonnaise, eg salad mixture or shellfish.

175g (6oz) mangetout, topped
  and tailed
1 red pepper, cored, deseeded and
  sliced
1 mooli, scrubbed and sliced
  thinly
110g (4oz) salad leaves, eg Iceberg
  lettuce or chinese leaves

Dressing:
6 × 15ml sp (6tbsp) cider
1 × 15ml sp (1tbsp) lemon juice
2 × 15ml sp (2tbsp) sunflower oil
2 × 15ml sp (2tbsp) apple juice

Red, White and Green Salad

1   Blanch the prepared mangetout in boiling salted water for 2 minutes. Drain and cool.
2   Prepare all the salad ingredients and place in a salad bowl with the mangetout.
3   Mix all the dressing ingredients together in a screw-topped jar. Pour the dressing over the salad and toss.

Note: Light, crisp and refreshing, the mooli is a variety of winter radish, available however all year round and identified by its smooth white skin and long tapering appearance. The flavour is milder than our red summer radish, slightly reminiscent of turnip with a more pungent smell. Mooli is also called great white radish, Japanese daikon or rettich and can be used raw in salads – it doesn't discolour on standing – or cooked when it retains its crisp, firm texture. It will keep in the refrigerator for up to two weeks.

Strawberry Cheese Tartlets

175g (6oz) plain flour
75g (3oz) butter
25g (1oz) caster sugar
3 egg yolks

Filling:
110g (4oz) cream cheese
3×15ml sp (3tbsp) greek yoghurt
225g (8oz) strawberries, hulled
  and sliced
4×15ml sp (4tbsp) redcurrant
  jelly

1   Rub the butter into the flour until it resembles fine breadcrumbs. Stir in the sugar and add the egg yolks. Add a little water if the mixture is dry. Gently knead dough until it comes together; chill.
2   Divide the pastry into four. Roll out and use to line 4 individual 11.5cm (4½in) loose-bottomed flan tins. Chill for 30 minutes.
3   Prick the base of each flan tin. Place a circle of greaseproof paper in each pastry case and fill with baking beans. Bake blind at 375°F (190°C), in the baking oven or near the bottom of the roasting oven, for 15 minutes. Remove beans and paper and return to the oven for 2 minutes. Cool and remove from the tins.
4   Mix together the cheese and the yoghurt and spoon into the cooled tartlet cases. Top with the sliced strawberries arranged in a circular pattern.
5   Gently warm the redcurrant jelly and spoon over the tartlets. Leave to cool and then serve.

Smoked Haddock Gougère

110g (4oz) unsalted butter
150ml (¼pt) water
110g (4oz) plain flour
salt and pepper
4 eggs
110g (4oz) gruyère cheese – finely
  grated
beaten egg to glaze
175g (6oz) smoked haddock
150ml (¼pt) milk
2 eggs, hard-boiled and chopped
15g (½oz) flour
15g (½oz) butter
1×2.5ml sp (½tsp) anchovy
  essence

1   Put the butter and water in a heavy based pan and bring to the boil. Immediately remove from the heat, add the flour and beat well with a wooden spoon. Return to a low heat and keep beating until the batter comes away easily from the sides of the pan and forms a glossy ball. Season to taste.
2   Remove from the heat and beat in the eggs one at a time, blending each thoroughly before adding the next. When ready the pastry will be smooth and glossy and stiff enough to hold its own shape when piped.
3   Beat most of the cheese into the pastry, leaving a little to sprinkle on the top.
4   Spoon the mixture in egg-sized mounds, one against the other, in a circle on a lightly greased baking sheet. Brush with the beaten egg and sprinkle with the remaining grated cheese. Bake at 400°F (200°C) or near the top of the roasting oven for about 30 minutes or until golden.
5   Meanwhile, poach the haddock in the milk in a moderate oven (beneath the gougère ring in the roasting oven) for 10–15 minutes. Remove from the milk and flake into a bowl; add the chopped hard-boiled eggs.
6   Place the milk in a pan with the flour and butter and cook gently over a low heat whisking all the time until thickened and smooth. Remove from the heat and add the anchovy essence. Pour onto the fish and mix well.
7   Lift the gougère onto a serving dish and pour the fish mixture into the centre. Serve at once.

450g (1lb) tomatoes
2 oranges
juice and rind of ½ orange
1×15ml sp (1tbsp) white wine
 vinegar
1×15ml sp (1tbsp) sunflower oil
2×15ml sp (2tbsp) fresh chopped
 basil
salt and pepper

150g (5oz) butter
150g (5oz) caster sugar
150g (5oz) ground almonds
150g (5oz) self-raising flour
1 egg
450g (1lb) cooking apples
1×5ml sp (1tsp) ground
 cinnamon
75g (3oz) soft brown sugar
225g (8oz) raspberries – fresh or
 frozen
cinnamon and icing sugar for
 dusting
greek yoghurt

Tomato Salad

1   Slice the tomatoes thinly. Peel and segment the oranges.
2   Mix together the remaining ingredients and place in a large bowl. Toss
    the tomatoes and oranges very carefully in the dressing and refrigerate
    for 1 hour. Toss again before serving.

Apple and Raspberry Torte

1   Place the butter, caster sugar, ground almonds, flour and egg in a bowl
    and beat well.
2   Grease a 21.5cm (8½in) diameter spring-release cake tin. Spread half
    the almond mixture into the tin, flattening it lightly with a fork.
3   Peel, core and chop the apples. Cook gently in a covered pan in their
    own juices, until just tender. Add the cinnamon and soft brown sugar.
    Cool slightly.
4   Spoon apples over the almond mixture, then the raspberries.
5   Dot over the remaining almond mixture so that it almost covers the
    fruit.
6   Stand the tin on a baking sheet and bake at 350°F (180°C) in the
    baking oven or on the grid shelf on the bottom of the roasting oven
    with the cold solid shelf on the top set of runners, for about 1 hour. The
    torte should feel just firm to the touch, with a springy texture. Leave to
    cool in the tin for 1 hour.
7   Dust with mixed cinnamon and icing sugar and serve warm
    accompanied by greek yoghurt.

Main Meals

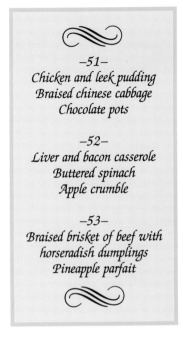

Chicken and Leek Pudding

1 Gently fry the bacon in its own fat until cooked. Remove with a slotted spoon and leave to drain on kitchen paper.
2 Mix the remaining filling ingredients together and add the bacon.
3 Mix together the flour, salt and suet for the pastry, and add enough water to make a soft dough.
4 Roll out and use two-thirds to line a greased 1 litre (2pt) pudding basin. Spoon in the filling, cover with a pastry lid made from the other one-third of pastry, and seal the edges well. Cover with greased greaseproof paper and foil.
5 Place the pudding in a pan containing sufficient boiling water to come halfway up the side of the basin. Steam on the boiling plate for 40–60 minutes before transferring to the simmering oven for 2½–3 hours. Alternatively, continue to cook on the simmering plate for a further 50–60 minutes.

110g (4oz) streaky bacon, rinded and chopped
340g (12oz) raw chicken flesh, roughly chopped
225g (8oz) leeks, washed and sliced
50g (2oz) button mushrooms, sliced
2×15ml sp (2tbsp) flour
salt and pepper
150ml (¼pt) chicken stock

Pastry:
225g (8oz) self-raising wholemeal flour
pinch salt
110g (4oz) shredded suet

Braised Chinese Cabbage

1 Fry the onions in the hot oil in a wok or a flameproof casserole for 1 minute.
2 Add the cabbage and stir over medium heat for 2 minutes.
3 Pour over the soy sauce and ginger wine and cook for a further 3 minutes. Serve immediately.

8 spring onions, chopped
2×15ml sp (2tbsp) vegetable oil
1 large chinese cabbage, chopped
1×15ml sp (1tbsp) light soy sauce
1×15ml sp (1tbsp) ginger wine

110g (4oz) white chocolate
600ml (1pt) milk
2 eggs
2 egg yolks
2×15ml sp (2tbsp) caster sugar

Chocolate Pots

1 Place the chocolate in a pan with the milk and simmer gently for 2 minutes, stirring occasionally.
2 Beat together the eggs, egg yolks and sugar, then pour on the chocolate milk. Blend well and strain into individual ovenproof pots or ramekins.
3 Place in a roasting tin containing 2.5cm (1in) of water. Bake at 350°F (180°C) in the baking oven or hung on the bottom set of runners in the roasting oven with the cold solid shelf on the top set of runners, for 35–40 minutes or until just set.
4 Remove from the pan, cool and chill before serving.

4 streaky bacon rashers, rinded and chopped
1 onion, chopped
450g (1lb) lambs' liver, sliced
2×15ml sp (2tbsp) wholemeal flour
1×400g (14oz) can tomatoes, chopped with their juices
300ml (½pt) beef stock
1×5ml sp (1tsp) sage
1×5ml sp (1tsp) worcestershire sauce
75g (3oz) mushrooms, sliced
salt and pepper

Liver and Bacon Casserole

1 Gently fry the bacon in a flameproof casserole until the fat runs, then add the chopped onion and cook gently until the onion is transparent. Remove from the casserole with a slotted spoon.
2 Toss the sliced liver in the flour and fry in the bacon fat until sealed.
3 Stir in the canned tomatoes, stock, sage and Worcestershire sauce. Add the mushrooms and the bacon and onion mixture, season and bake at 350°F (180°C), in the baking oven or at the bottom of the roasting oven, for 30 minutes. Serve hot.

900g (2lb) fresh spinach
25g (1oz) butter
1×2.5ml sp (½tsp) grated nutmeg
salt and pepper

Buttered Spinach

1 Wash spinach thoroughly, shake off excess water and place in a large heavy-based pan. Cover and cook gently for 6–8 minutes.
2 Drain away any water left at the end of the cooking period, return the spinach to the pan with the butter and heat over gentle heat until the butter has melted. Stir butter into the spinach with the nutmeg and seasoning. Serve immediately.

675g (1½lb) cooking apples
75g (3oz) raisins
50–75g (2–3oz) sugar
2×5ml sp (2tsp) cinnamon
50g (2oz) self-raising wholemeal flour
110g (4oz) jumbo rolled oats
50g (2oz) demerara sugar
110g (4oz) melted butter

Apple Crumble

1 Peel and slice the apples and cook gently with the raisins and a little water until soft. Add sugar to taste and cinnamon, and place in a deep ovenproof dish.
2 Mix together the flour, oats and sugar and gradually add the melted butter; spread over the apple mixture.
3 Bake at 400°F (200°C) or near the top of the roasting oven, for 30 minutes. Serve hot or cold.

Braised Brisket of Beef with Horseradish Dumplings

1.4–1.8kg (3–4lb) boned and rolled brisket
225g (8oz) carrots, chopped
225g (8oz) leeks, washed and sliced thickly
1 bunch of fresh herbs, eg parsley, thyme, marjoram and a bay leaf, or 1×5ml sp (1tsp) mixed dried herbs
salt and pepper
600ml (1pt) cider or red wine
oil for frying
600ml (1pt) boiling water

Horseradish dumplings:
110g (4oz) self-raising wholemeal flour
50g (2oz) shredded suet
salt and pepper
water to mix
3×5ml sp (3tsp) freshly grated or 6×5ml sp (6tsp) creamed, horseradish

1 Place the beef in a large bowl and put the prepared vegetables over and around it.
2 Tie the fresh herbs in a bunch and lay on the beef, or sprinkle the dried herbs over it.
3 Add a little salt and pepper to the cider or wine and pour over the meat and vegetables. Leave for at least 4 hours or, preferably, overnight. Spoon the liquid over the meat from time to time and turn over the beef at least once.
4 Heat a little oil in a large wide cast-iron casserole on the boiling plate and briefly fry the drained beef on all sides to seal in the juices. Remove from the casserole and add the drained vegetables. Place the beef back on the top and pour over the marinade. Add the boiling water; it should come halfway up the joint.
5 Cover tightly and cook at 250°F (120°C) or on the bottom of the simmering oven, for 4 hours.
6 Meanwhile make the dumplings. Mix together the flour, suet and salt and pepper and add sufficient water to make a soft dough.
7 Turn out onto a floured board and with lightly floured hands shape into balls about the size of large walnuts. With a finger, make a hollow in each and put a portion of either the fresh or creamed horseradish into each hollow. Squeeze the dough over it to seal it tightly.
8 If the casserole is sufficiently large, pop the dumplings round the beef 20 minutes before the end of the cooking period and transfer to the bottom of the roasting oven on the grid shelf (375°F, 190°C) for 15–20 minutes. Alternatively, remove the beef from the casserole once cooked and keep warm while the dumplings are cooked in the cooking liquid as above.
9 Serve the meat sliced with the vegetables and dumplings.

Pineapple Parfait

225ml (8oz) natural set yoghurt
1×15ml sp (1tsp) clear honey
225g (8oz) fresh pineapple flesh, chopped
225g (8oz) fresh strawberries, hulled

1 Mix together the yoghurt and honey, place in a shallow freezer-proof container and freeze until just firm.
2 Transfer to a food processor or blender and mix well.
3 Add the chopped pineapple and blend.
4 Return to the container and freeze for 2 hours or until firm. Scoop out and serve with the strawberries.

Note: This dessert is best made the day it is to be eaten or it may become hard and icy.

450g (1lb) minced beef
1 large onion, chopped
1 large carrot, sliced thinly
1×15ml sp (1tbsp) flour
1×5ml sp (1tsp) mixed herbs
1×15ml sp (1tbsp) fresh chopped
  parsley
1×15ml sp (1tbsp) tomato purée
300ml (½pt) beef stock

Topping:
900g (2lb) potatoes
2 large leeks, sliced
50g (2oz) butter
salt and pepper

Special Cottage Pie *colour below*

1　Fry the meat, onion and carrot together until the onion is soft. Stir in the flour, mixed herbs, parsley and purée, add the beef stock. Cover and cook for 45 minutes. Alternatively, cover and place in the simmering oven for 1½ hours.
2　Boil the potatoes in salted water; boil the sliced leeks for 10 minutes and drain well.
3　Mash the potatoes and stir in the butter. Season to taste.
4　Place the meat mixture in a pie dish, spread the leeks on top and pipe the mashed potato over the top. Bake at 400°F (200°C) or near the top of the roasting oven for about 25 minutes, until nicely browned.

Note: Cooked minced beef may be used, in which case it should only be cooked for 10 minutes after adding the stock.

French Beans

These are sometimes called dwarf beans, haricot verts or bobby beans.

　Top and tail them with scissors and cook in boiling salted water for about 5 minutes if they are really tiny, 10–12 minutes if larger. They can be tossed in a little olive oil and crushed garlic before serving.

Special Cottage Pie and Monday Pie – page 58 (Cadbury Schweppes)

Hot Chocolate Trifle

1. Slice the swiss roll and arrange over the base and sides of a 900ml (1½pt) soufflé type ovenproof dish.
2. Spoon a little of the fruit juice over the swiss roll. Then spoon in the fruit.
3. Blend together the cornflour, egg yolks, sugar and a little of the milk. Heat the remaining milk until just boiling, pour onto the cornflour mixture and stir well. Return to the pan and heat gently until boiling, stirring all the time. Cook for 1–2 minutes to thicken, then pour over the apricots.
4. Whisk the egg whites until stiff; whisk in half the sugar then gently fold in the other half. Pipe or spoon on top of the custard, sprinkle over the almonds and bake at 350°F (180°C) in the baking oven or at the bottom of the roasting oven, for 20–25 minutes or until nicely browned. Serve immediately.

1 chocolate swiss roll
1×410g (14½oz) can apricot
 halves in natural juice, drained
2×15ml sp (2tbsp) cornflour
2 eggs, separated
1×15ml sp (1tbsp) sugar
600ml (1pt) milk
110g (4oz) caster sugar
25g (1oz) flaked almonds

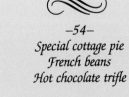

–54–
Special cottage pie
French beans
Hot chocolate trifle

–56–
Skate wings with fennel
Sweet potatoes with apples
Queen of puddings

4 skate wings
2 heads of fennel
300ml (½pt) apple juice
salt and pepper

Skate Wings with Fennel

1 Rinse the skate well and dry thoroughly. Place in a lightly greased shallow ovenproof dish.
2 Trim off stem tops and slice off the base of the fennel, and wash well. Cut into quarters and slice thinly. Scatter over the top of the skate wings.
3 Pour over the apple juice and season lightly. Bake at 350°F (180°C) in the baking oven or on the grid shelf on the bottom of the roasting oven for 20–30 minutes.

    Serve immediately with rice or sweet potatoes either cooked in their jackets (scrubbed and cooked for 1–1½ hours in a hot oven) or cooked with apples as in the creole dish which follows.

450g (1lb) sweet potatoes
450g (1lb) cooking apples
50g (2oz) butter
1×5ml sp (1tsp) salt
50g (2oz) soft brown sugar
1×5ml sp (1tsp) nutmeg
1×15ml sp (1tbsp) lemon juice

Sweet Potatoes with Apples

1 Peel and thinly slice the sweet potatoes; peel, core and thinly slice the apples.
2 Butter a deep casserole dish and arrange in it alternate layers of potato and apples, starting and finishing with sweet potatoes. Sprinkle each layer with salt, sugar, nutmeg and lemon juice and dot with the remaining butter.
3 Cover the casserole and bake at 400°F (200°C) or in the centre of the roasting oven for 30 minutes. Remove the lid and cook for a further 15–20 minutes or until the potatoes are tender. Serve straight from the casserole.

600ml (1pt) milk
25g (1oz) butter
1 orange, grated rind and juice
150g (5oz) fresh white or brown
  breadcrumbs
150g (5oz) caster sugar
4 eggs, separated
4×15ml sp (4tbsp) apricot jam

Queen of Puddings

1 Slowly heat the milk and butter together on the simmering plate until the butter is melted and the milk lukewarm. Remove from heat and add orange rind.
2 Mix together the breadcrumbs and 25g (1oz) of the sugar in a bowl and pour onto the milk. Leave to stand for 10–15 minutes then beat in the egg yolks.
3 Grease a 2-litre (4pt) shallow ovenproof dish and pour in the custard. Bake at 350°F (180°C) on the grid shelf on the base of the roasting oven with the cold solid shelf on the top set of runners, or in the baking oven, for 30 minutes or until the top is just set. Alternatively, bake in a water bath in the simmering oven for about 1 hour until set.
4 Combine the apricot jam and the orange juice (use only half the orange if large) and spread over the pudding carefully.
5 Whisk the egg whites until stiff, then whisk in remaining sugar. Spoon or pipe over the top of the pudding and bake at 350°F (180°C) in the baking oven or on the grid shelf at the bottom of the roasting oven protected by the solid shelf, for 15–20 minutes or until pale golden brown. Serve immediately.

Spiced Lamb with Apricots

1.1kg (2½lb) lean leg of lamb, boned
2×15ml sp (2tbsp) sunflower oil
1 onion, chopped
1 clove garlic
1×5ml sp (1tsp) ground coriander
1×5ml sp (1tsp) ground ginger
1×5ml sp (1tsp) mild chilli powder
pinch ground cardamom
1×15ml sp (1tbsp) flour
300ml (½pt) stock
salt and pepper
50g (2oz) no-soak dried apricots
175g (6oz) small okra

1   Cut the lamb into 4cm (1½in) cubes and lightly brown in the oil. Remove and keep warm in the simmering oven.
2   Soften the onion and garlic in the same pan, then add all the spices; cook for 2 minutes. Stir in the flour and gradually add the stock and seasoning. Pour over the meat, cover and cook at 325°F (160°C) or in the simmering oven for 1½ hours.
3   Roughly chop the apricots. Trim away the conical cap from the stalk end of the okra and trim the tail end. Cut into 4cm (1½in) lengths if they are large. Add to the casserole and cook for a further 15 minutes or until the okra are just tender.

Sometimes known as 'ladies' fingers', okra is available all year round in many of the larger supermarkets as well as in ethnic shops. Okra can be used whole, or sliced where the juice is used as a thickening agent. It does not require much cooking and is best eaten *al dente*, but may be softened by longer cooking. However, overcooking will make it soft, stringy and shapeless. Its flavour blends well with tomatoes, seafood and chicken.

Baked Marrow with Tomato and Basil

1×15ml sp (1tbsp) vegetable oil
1 bunch spring onions, chopped
1 clove garlic, crushed
4 ripe tomatoes, skinned and chopped
675g (1½lb) marrow
1×15ml sp (1tbsp) fresh chopped basil or 1×5ml sp (1tsp) dried basil
salt and pepper

1   Heat the oil in a cast-iron casserole and gently soften the onions and garlic. Stir in the chopped tomatoes and cook for a further 5 minutes.
2   Cut the marrow into 4cm (1½in) chunks leaving the peel on, add to the tomatoes and onions with the basil and seasoning. Stir well.
3   Place the lid on the casserole and cook at 300°F (150°C) or in the simmering oven for about 1 hour or until the marrow is tender.
4   About 10 minutes before the end of the cooking period put the casserole back on the simmering plate and simmer without the lid on to reduce the liquid. Serve hot or cold, with boiled rice.

Sussex Pond Pudding

225g (8oz) self-raising flour
110g (4oz) shredded suet
1×5ml sp (1tsp) grated lemon rind
110g (4oz) butter, diced
110g (4oz) demerara sugar
1 large lemon, washed and pricked all over

Lemon Sauce
110g (4oz) caster sugar
1×15ml sp (1tbsp) cornflour
250ml (9fl oz) water
grated rind of 1 lemon
25g (1oz) unsalted butter cut into small pieces
3×15ml sp (3tbsp) lemon juice

1   Mix together the flour, suet and lemon rind and add sufficient water to bind to a soft dough. Turn out onto a floured board and knead gently until free of cracks.
2   On a floured board, roll out the pastry into a large circle and with a sharp knife cut out a quarter segment of the circle to use as a lid. Use the remaining pastry to line a greased 900ml (1½pt) pudding basin; damp the cut edges and press to seal.
3   Gently mix together the butter and sugar. Half fill the lined basin and press the lemon into the centre. Cover with the remaining butter and sugar.
4   Roll the reserved quarter of pastry into a circle, dampen the edges and put it on top of the filling, pressing the edges together to seal.
5   Cover with greased greaseproof paper and foil, making a pleat across the top to allow for expansion. Tie down with string.   (cont)

6   Steam either in a steamer or in a pan containing sufficient water to come halfway up the sides of the basin, for 2½ hours.
7   To serve, carefully invert onto a hot shallow serving dish and serve hot with cream or a lemon sauce.

Lemon Sauce
1   Place the sugar and cornflour in a pan and gradually add the water, mixing to a smooth paste. Stir in the grated lemon rind and cook gently over a low heat, stirring all the time until the mixture thickens. Continue simmering for about 1 minute.
2   Remove from the heat and beat in the butter pieces one at a time. Stir in the lemon juice and serve.

Note: The name of this pudding is derived from the 'pond' of buttery sauce which oozes out when the pudding is cut. Make sure when serving the pudding that all receive a small piece of the cooked lemon.

340g (12oz) cold roast beef
75g (3oz) onions
1×400g (14oz) can tomatoes with their juices
1×440g (15oz) can baked beans
1×15ml sp (1tbsp) wholegrain mustard
salt and pepper
450g (1lb) potatoes, either cold roast or parboiled, sliced
75g (3oz) cheddar cheese, grated (optional)

Monday Pie *colour page 54*

1   Mince the cold roast beef and onions together into a basin. Stir in the tomatoes, baked beans and mustard. Season and turn into a 900ml (1½pt) shallow ovenproof dish.
2   Arrange the sliced potatoes on top of the meat and sprinkle with the grated cheese.
3   Bake at 375°F (190°C) or in the centre of the roasting oven, for 30–40 minutes.

225h (8oz) ripe plums
225g (8oz) cooking or dessert apples
50g (2oz) unsalted butter
1×2.5ml (¼tsp) ground cloves
110g (4oz) caster sugar
4 eggs, separated
4×15ml sp (4tbsp) double cream

Plum and Apple Tansy *colour opposite*

1   Halve the plums and remove the stones. Peel, core and slice the apples. Cook the fruit with the butter over gentle heat, adding a little water if they threaten to burn, until the fruit is pulpy.
2   Remove from the heat and rub through a sieve or use food processor.
3   Return the purée to the pan and stir in the cloves, sugar and beaten egg yolks. Whisk the egg whites until stiff but not dry and fold carefully into the fruit and egg mixture. Cook over a low heat, stirring gently until the tansy is quite thick.
4   Allow the mixture to cool and then pour into individual glasses; chill in the refrigerator for 1 hour.
5   Serve with the whipped double cream.

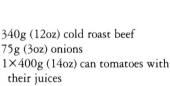

Plum and Apple Tansy and Baked Apples with Apricots – page 32 (Kenwood)

Note: The name 'tansy' derives from the bitter-tasting herb once used to flavour this dish, but it now describes a buttered fruit and egg purée.

675g (1½lb) fresh spinach
1 small onion
1 × 15ml sp (1tbsp) vegetable oil
110g (4oz) breadcrumbs
110g (4oz) cheddar cheese, grated
1 egg
salt and pepper
grated nutmeg
milk to mix

Spinach Castles (serves 6)

1 Cook the spinach in a large pan of boiling salted water until just tender; be careful not to overcook or the leaves will disintegrate. Drain and press between two plates to remove excess water. In this way the delicate leaves remain whole and unbroken.
2 Carefully use two-thirds of the spinach leaves to line 6 greased dariole moulds allowing sufficient excess to make lids on top of the filling. Chop the remaining spinach very finely.
3 Soften the onion in the oil and mix with the breadcrumbs, cheese and chopped spinach. Add the egg, seasoning and nutmeg and sufficient milk to bind.
4 Press the stuffing firmly into the dariole moulds and cover the tops with the folded-over spinach leaves.
5 Cover with greased greaseproof paper or foil and bake in a roasting tin half-filled with boiling water at 350°F (180°C) in the centre of the baking oven, or hung on the bottom set of runners in the roasting oven with the cold solid shelf on the top set of runners, for 30–40 minutes.
6 When cooked, carefully turn out onto a warm serving dish.

50g (2oz) whole almonds, skinned and chopped
50g (2oz) medium oatmeal
300ml (½pt) double cream
1 × 15ml sp (1tbsp) lemon juice
4 × 15ml sp (4tbsp) whisky
2 × 15ml sp (2tbsp) clear honey
lemon twists to decorate

Atholl Brose (serves 6)

1 Place the almonds and oatmeal on a baking tray and grill near the top of the roasting oven until brown, turning frequently. Leave to cool.
2 Whip the cream until it stands in soft peaks, then carefully whisk in the lemon juice, whisky and honey.
3 Fold in the cooled almonds and oatmeal.
4 Spoon into 6 glasses and chill.
5 Serve decorated with lemon twists.

900g (2lb) spare ribs
5 × 15ml sp (5tbsp) tomato purée
2 × 15ml sp (2tbsp) soy sauce
1 × 15ml sp (1tbsp) clear honey
3 × 15ml sp (3tbsp) red wine vinegar
450ml (¾pt) beef stock
salt and pepper

Barbecued Spare Ribs *colour opposite*

1 Place the ribs in a single layer in a large ovenproof dish.
2 Whisk together the remaining ingredients and pour over the ribs (they should be covered by the sauce). Leave to marinade for several hours or overnight in a refrigerator.
3 Bake at 400°F (200°C) or near the top of the roasting oven for 30 minutes, then at 350°F (180°C) in the baking oven or at the bottom of the roasting oven covered with foil for a further 1 hour. Alternatively, place in the simmering oven (300°F, 150°C) after the initial roasting and cook for a further 2 hours.

450g (1lb) curly kale or spring
  green cabbage, shredded
110g (4oz) spring onions, chopped
  including the green
110g (4oz) peas
50g (2oz) bean sprouts
1 × 15ml sp (1tbsp) vegetable oil
  (sunflower, groundnut or soya)
2 × 15ml sp (2tbsp) ginger wine
1 × 15ml sp (1tbsp) soy sauce

Crispy Green Stir-Fry

1 Prepare the vegetables. Heat the oil in a wok or large skillet and, when it is very hot, add the vegetables and stir continuously for 3 minutes with the pan still on the boiling plate.

2 Mix together the ginger wine and soy sauce and pour over the vegetables. Cook on a high heat for a further 1 minute. Serve immediately.

Note: Stir-frying uses more heat and less oil than sautéing. The vegetables taking longest to cook are always put in first, while flavourings are added last to enhance the taste. Liquid flavourings generate a burst of steam which finishes cooking the vegetables. The wok is the traditional pan for stir-frying, its thin metal shape ensuring that the heat is evenly distributed with the largest area possible available for cooking. A large frying pan can be used instead.

Variations
Any combination of vegetables and flavourings can be used and not necessarily Chinese.

–61–
Wiltshire plait
Spinach castles
Atholl brose

–62–
Barbecued spare ribs
Crispy green stir-fry
Pineapple chiffon flan

225g (8oz) digestive biscuits
110g (4oz) butter
2×5ml sp (2tsp) powdered
  gelatine
3×15ml sp (3tbsp) water
3 eggs, separated
175g (6oz) caster sugar
1 can crushed pineapple or 400g
  (14oz) fresh pineapple
1 lemon, grated rind and juice
225g (8oz) low-fat soft cheese
cream and pineapple pieces to
  garnish

Pineapple Chiffon Flan

1 Crush biscuits and mix with the melted butter. Use to make a shell in a 25cm (10in) loose-bottomed tart tin.
2 Sprinkle the gelatine over the water and leave to soak.
3 Beat the egg yolks with 50g (2oz) of the sugar until pale, add the pineapple, lemon rind and juice. Turn into a saucepan and cook gently on the simmering plate, without boiling, until thick.
4 Blend in the soaked gelatine, then the cheese. Cool until on the point of setting.
5 Whisk the egg whites stiffly and gradually whisk in 75g (3oz) of the sugar. When mixture stands in firm peaks, whisk in the remaining 25g (1oz) sugar and the pineapple cheese.
6 Pile into the biscuit shell and chill.
7 To serve, remove flan ring and decorate with cream and fresh pineapple pieces.

340g (12oz) smoked haddock
1 bunch spring onions, chopped
110g (4oz) button mushrooms,
  sliced
75g (3oz) sweetcorn
1×400g (14oz) can tomatoes,
  chopped with juice
salt and pepper
110g (4oz) jumbo oats
75g (3oz) cheddar cheese, grated

Smoked Haddock Crumble

1 Skin the fish and chop into 5cm (2in) pieces. Place in a shallow ovenproof dish with the chopped spring onions, sliced mushrooms, sweetcorn and canned tomatoes. Season lightly (the fish may be very salty).
2 Sprinkle over the jumbo oats and the grated cheese and bake at 375°F (190°C) or on the grid shelf on the base of the roasting oven for 30 minutes, or until the cheese has started to brown. Serve at once, with Broccoli Fritters.

450g (1lb) broccoli
oil for deep frying, preferably
  groundnut oil but any vegetable
  oil will do
2 egg whites
2×15ml sp (2tbsp) plain flour
salt and pepper

Broccoli Fritters

1 Prepare the broccoli by trimming off the stalks to leave just the sprigs. Wash well and dry.
2 Fill a deep-fat fryer or large saucepan to a third of its capacity with the oil, and heat it up to 360°F (185°C) — or until a cube of bread turns golden in 60 seconds.
3 Whisk the egg whites until stiff.
4 Coat the broccoli sprigs in the flour and then in the beaten egg white. Deep fry in 2 batches, shaking the pan gently and using a knife to keep the sprigs apart. They should only need 2–3 minutes cooking. Drain on crumpled greaseproof paper and serve immediately or they will lose their crispness.

Loganberry Mousse

1 Strain juice from fruit and make up to 275ml (½pt) with water. Bring to the boil in a pan, add jelly and stir until dissolved; leave until nearly set.
2 Sieve loganberries.
3 Whisk the cold evaporated milk together with the lemon juice until thick, then fold in the setting jelly and fruit purée. Pour into a bowl and leave until set.

1×411g (14½oz) can
  loganberries
1 packet raspberry jelly
1×175g (6oz) can evaporated
  milk, chilled
1×15ml sp (1tsp) lemon juice

Beef Casserole with Herby Dumplings (David & Charles)

110g (4oz) aduki beans
450g (1lb) braising steak
2×15ml sp (2tbsp) vegetable oil
1 large onion, sliced
1×15ml sp (1tbsp) flour
2×15ml sp (2tbsp) redcurrant
  jelly
300ml (½pt) beef stock
300ml (½pt) Guinness
175g (6oz) button mushrooms
salt and pepper

110g (4oz) self-raising wholemeal
  flour
50g (2oz) shredded suet
salt and pepper
½×15ml sp (½tsp) dried herbs
or 1×15ml sp (1tsp) fresh herbs
water to mix

450g (1lb) broccoli
225g (8oz) celeriac
a little lemon juice
25g (1oz) sesame seeds

Beef Casserole with Beans *colour opposite*

1 Soak the beans overnight, then boil for 10 minutes in fresh water.
2 Cut the meat into 5cm (2in) cubes. Heat the oil in a pan and seal the meat quickly, remove meat from pan. Add the onion and cook until soft.
3 Stir in the flour and cook for 1 minute. Add the redcurrant jelly, beef stock and beer and bring to the boil.
4 Add the sealed meat, the whole button mushrooms, the partially cooked beans and seasoning. Transfer to the simmering oven, 300°F (150°C) for 2–2½ hours. Alternatively place on the grid shelf on the bottom of the roasting oven for 1–1½ hours at 350°F (180°C).

Note: Many different types of bean can be used in this casserole including flageolet (very young green haricot beans), pinto beans, red kidney beans and mung beans.

Variation:
Omit beans and serve with Herby Dumplings.

Herby Dumplings

1 Mix together the dry ingredients and add sufficient water to bind to a firm dough.
2 Divide the mixture into 8–10 pieces and shape each into a ball.
3 Drop balls into the cooking liquid ½ hour before the end of the cooking time. If cooking the casserole in the simmering oven, move to the bottom of the roasting oven when adding the dumplings.

Broccoli and Celeriac

1 Trim off any tough or fibrous ends from the broccoli stalks and wash well. Halve the stalks and heads lengthwise if large.
2 Peel the celeriac and cut into even-sized chunks. Plunge into cold water, mixed with a little lemon juice, to prevent browning.
3 Steam celeriac for 15–20 minutes. If there is sufficient room, add the broccoli with the celeriac for the last 10 minutes; if not, steam separately and carefully mix with the celeriac when cooked.
4 Serve immediately with the sesame seeds sprinkled on top.

Note: Celeriac looks rather like a turnip but has the flavour of celery and can be used in cookery whenever a gentle celery flavour is required. It can be eaten raw in salads or steamed, boiled or puréed. The flesh browns quickly on exposure to air so plunge into acidulated water or, if used raw for a salad, stir straight into the dressing.

175g (6oz) plain flour
pinch salt
75g (3oz) butter
25g (1oz) sugar
2 egg yolks
25g (1oz) plain flour
150g (5oz) soft brown sugar
225g (8oz) soured cream or greek
  yoghurt
450g (1lb) cooking apples, peeled,
  cored and sliced
175g (6oz) blackberries

Apple and Blackberry Cream Pie

1 Mix flour and salt in a bowl and rub in the butter until the mixture resembles breadcrumbs. Add the sugar and egg yolks and stir with a knife until a dough forms. Knead lightly until smooth. Cover and chill for 30 minutes.
2 Use pastry to line a 18cm (7in) deep-sided loose-bottomed flan tin.
3 Beat together the flour, 110g (4oz) of the sugar and the cream or yoghurt until well mixed and smooth.
4 Arrange apple slices and blackberries in the pastry case and pour the cream mixture over the top. Sprinkle over the remaining sugar and bake at 450°F (230°C) or near the top of the roasting oven for 15 minutes. Reduce the heat and cook for another 30 minutes at 350°F (180°C) on the grid shelf at the bottom of the roasting oven with the cold solid shelf on the top set of runners, or in the baking oven, until set and browned. Serve immediately.

Variations:
This pie can be made with any fruits but add an additional 25g (1oz) of flour when soft fruits such as raspberries or strawberries are used.

340g (12oz) lean mince
75g (3oz) jumbo oats
1×15ml sp (1tbsp) tomato purée
2×15ml sp (2tbsp) sweet pickle
1×5ml sp (1tsp) wholegrain
  mustard
1 egg
salt and pepper
50g (2oz) mushrooms, sliced
50g (2oz) cheddar cheese, grated
1×397g (14oz) can tinned
  tomatoes or
½ a jar of passatta

Layered Meat Loaf

1 Mix together the mince, oats, tomato purée, pickle, mustard and egg and season well. Place half the mixture in the bottom of a greased 450g (1lb) loaf tin and press down evenly.
2 Place the sliced mushrooms on the top followed by the cheese; pack down firmly.
3 Finally add the rest of the meat mixture and again press down firmly.
4 Cover the loaf tin with foil and bake at 375°F (190°C) or in the centre of the roasting oven for 50–60 minutes.
5 Make tomato sauce by puréeing the canned tomatoes with their juices, sieving to remove the pips and then gently heating; the passatta just needs heating.
6 Turn out the meat loaf and serve with the warmed tomato sauce.

25g (1oz) butter
2 bunches spring onions
450g (1lb) frozen peas
salt

Lyonnaise Peas

1 Melt the butter in a small pan and add the spring onions; soften over a gentle heat for 2–3 minutes.
2 Meanwhile, bring a pan of salted water to the boil, add the peas and cook for 3 minutes on the simmering plate.
3 Drain the peas and mix with the onions. Serve hot.

Pear Flan

1 Rub the butter into the flour until the mixture resembles fine bread-crumbs, stir in sugar. Add the egg yolks and a little water to bind; chill.

2 Roll out pastry and line a 21.5cm (8½in) loose-bottomed fluted tart tin; chill.

3 Line the pastry case with greaseproof paper and fill with beans. Bake blind at 375°F (190°C) or in the centre of the roasting oven for 10 minutes. Remove beans and paper and return flan case to the oven for a further 2 minutes to dry out the base.

4 Whisk together the whole egg, 25g (1oz) of demerara sugar, cheese, milk and nutmeg.

5 Peel pears, halve and scoop out the cores. Slice lengthwise and fan out in the flan case. Pour over the custard mixture, sprinkle with the breadcrumbs and remaining demerara sugar and bake at 350°F (180°C) in the roasting oven on the grid shelf with the cold solid shelf on the top set of runners or in the baking oven for 30 minutes or until the custard is set. Serve warm.

75g (3oz) butter
175g (6oz) plain flour
1×15ml sp (1tbsp) caster sugar
2 egg yolks
1 egg
75g (3oz) demerara sugar
50g (2oz) low-fat soft cheese
2×15ml sp (2tbsp) milk
1×5ml sp (1tsp) ground nutmeg
450g (1lb) even-sized ripe pears
  (about 3)
25g (1oz) breadcrumbs

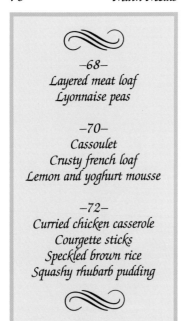

*Cassoulet and French Onion Soup
– page 82 (Kenwood)*

340g (12oz) haricot beans
450g (1lb) piece belly pork, boned
   and cut into strips
225g (½lb) piece streaky bacon,
   chopped into large pieces
4 cloves garlic
4 sticks celery
salt and pepper
1 bayleaf
1 sprig each of thyme, parsley and
   rosemary
6 juniper berries, crushed
2×5ml sp (2tsp) made mustard
6 small joints (goose, chicken,
   duck or rabbit)
225g (8oz) garlic sausage (or pork)
150g (5oz) breadcrumbs

50ml (2fl oz) milk
4 eggs, separated
110g (4oz) caster sugar
1×2.5ml sp (½tsp) vanilla
   essence
5×5ml sp (5tsp) powdered
   gelatine
450ml (¾pt) natural yoghurt
juice of 1 lemon
150ml (5fl oz) whipping cream
1×400g (14oz) can peach slices in
   natural juice

Cassoulet *colour opposite*

1   It is not necessary to soak the beans overnight. Just wash them well in two changes of water and place them in a saucepan with about 1.75 litres (3pt) of water. Bring to the boil and simmer for 2 minutes, then leave to soak for an hour in the cooking liquid.

2   Drain beans and place in a large deep casserole. Add all the other ingredients except the meat joints, sausage and breadcrumbs. Cover with cold water, put on the lid and place on the bottom of the roasting oven for 30 minutes (375°F, 190°C). Then reduce the heat to 300°F (150°C) or place in the simmering oven for 5–6 hours, checking the liquid level and adding more water if necessary.

3   Add the meat joints, pushing them well down into the beans and cook at the same temperature for a further 1½ hours.

4   Add the cut-up garlic sausage and sprinkle with the breadcrumbs. Place in the roasting oven for 30–40 minutes or until the top is nice and brown and the sausage cooked. Serve straight from the pot, with a crusty french loaf.

Lemon and Yoghurt Mousse

1   Scald the milk in a small pan. Cream the egg yolks and 25g (1oz) of the sugar in a small bowl until pale in colour. Gradually add the milk, mixing well. Return to the pan and stir constantly over low heat on the simmering plate until the mixture begins to thicken and just coats the back of the spoon. Do not allow to boil or the mixture will coagulate. Pour into a large bowl and add the vanilla essence.

2   Sprinkle the gelatine over 4×15ml sp (4tbsp) water in a bowl and leave to soak. Dissolve by standing in a pan of simmering water; cool, then add to the custard.

(cont)

TODAYS
SPECIAL

FRENCH
ONION
SOUP
&
CASSOULET

3 Whisk in the yoghurt and strained lemon juice. Leave until cool and thick but not set.
4 Whisk the egg whites until stiff and fold in the remaining sugar. Lightly whip the cream and fold into the yoghurt mixture with the meringue. Pour into a large glass serving dish, cover and chill until set – about 3 hours.
5 Purée the peaches and juices until smooth. Serve separately.

1 onion, sliced
1×15ml sp (1tbsp) sunflower oil
1 clove garlic, crushed
1×5ml sp (1tsp) curry powder
1×2.5ml sp (½tsp) ground ginger
1×2.5ml sp (½tsp) turmeric
1×15ml sp (1tbsp) flour
300ml (½pt) chicken stock
4 chicken joints, skinned
salt and pepper
110g (4oz) cooked and peeled prawns

Curried Chicken Casserole

1 Gently fry the onion in the oil in a flameproof casserole until soft. Add the garlic, curry powder and ginger and cook gently for 2 minutes on the simmering plate.
2 Add the turmeric and the flour followed by the chicken stock and bring to the boil.
3 Add the skinned chicken joints and seasoning to the casserole and bake at 350°F (180°C) or in the centre of the roasting oven for 1 hour. Alternatively, once the casserole is boiling, place on the grid shelf at the bottom of the simmering oven for 2–3 hours.
4 About 5 minutes before serving, stir in the prawns.

450g (1lb) courgettes
25g (1oz) butter
pinch nutmeg
salt and pepper

Courgette Sticks

1 Wash, top and tail the courgettes and cut into matchsticks.
2 Put the prepared courgettes into a 900ml (1½pt) ovenproof dish with sufficient water just to cover the bottom. Dot with the butter, sprinkle with the nutmeg and seasoning.
3 Cover with foil and cook in the simmering oven for 30–60 minutes according to taste.

175g (6oz) brown rice
1 small red pepper, cored, seeded and chopped
25g (1oz) pine nuts

Speckled Brown Rice

1 Wash the rice thoroughly and put into a large pan of boiling salted water. Transfer to the simmering plate and cook for 15–20 minutes.
2 Strain and rinse thoroughly with warm water.
3 Put in an ovenproof dish and stir in the diced pepper and pine nuts.
4 Cover with foil and place in the simmering oven to dry and keep warm until required.

Squashy Rhubarb Pudding

110g (4oz) butter
175g (6oz) self-raising flour
50g (2oz) sugar
grated rind of 1 orange
225g (8oz) fresh rhubarb
110g (4oz) butter
110g (4oz) caster sugar
2 eggs
110g (4oz) self-raising flour
1×15ml (1tbsp) orange juice
25g (1oz) sugar

1 Rub the butter into the flour until it resembles fine breadcrumbs, stir in the sugar and orange rind.
2 Prepare rhubarb; cut it into 2.5cm (1in) lengths.
3 Cream together the butter and 110g (4oz) sugar until light and fluffy. Beat in eggs, a little at a time, then fold in the flour. Carefully add the orange juice.
4 Pour into a greased 20cm (8in) cake tin and spread flat. Cover with the rhubarb pieces sprinkled with the 25g (1oz) sugar followed by the crumble mixture.
5 Bake at 375°F (190°C) or at the bottom of the roasting oven for 45 minutes. Allow to cool in the tin. Serve warm or cold.

Lamb Shrewsbury

8 lamb cutlets from best end of neck or loin chops
110g (4oz) button mushrooms, sliced
4×15ml sp (4tbsp) redcurrant jelly
2×15ml sp (2tbsp) Worcestershire sauce
juice of 1 lemon
1×15ml sp (1tbsp) flour
300ml (½pt) stock or red wine
freshly grated nutmeg
salt and pepper

1 Brown the chops in their own fat on both sides. Place in a casserole with the mushrooms.
2 Put the redcurrant jelly, Worcestershire sauce and lemon juice in a pan. Stir over gentle heat until the jelly is melted and all the ingredients combined.
3 Stir the flour into the meat fat and juices in the pan and cook for 1 minute. Then stir in the jelly mixture and the stock or wine to make a thickened sauce.
4 Season with nutmeg and salt and pepper and pour over the lamb. Bake at 300°F (150°C) in the simmering oven for 2–3 hours. Serve hot.

Parsnip Croquettes

675g (1½lb) parsnips
salt and pepper
50g (2oz) low-fat soft cheese
1 egg yolk
1 egg
110g (4oz) stale brown breadcrumbs

1 Peel the parsnips, cut into chunks and cook in boiling salted water until tender. Drain well.
2 Mash, then beat in the cheese and egg yolk. Allow to cool.
3 With floured hands, shape the parsnip mixture into dumpy logs about 6.5cm (2½in) in length. Place on a baking sheet and chill for 15 minutes.
4 Lightly beat the egg, coat the croquettes, then coat with the crumbs and chill for a further 15 minutes.
5 Place the baking sheet near the top of the roasting oven and grill for about 7 minutes, turning frequently, until evenly golden brown.

Note: These croquettes may be frozen at the end of stage 4. Just thaw overnight in the refrigerator and cook as above.

225g (8oz) self-raising flour
3×15ml sp (3tbsp) cocoa
110g (4oz) caster sugar
75g (3oz) butter
225ml (8fl oz) milk
1×2.5ml sp (½tsp) vanilla
  essence
110g (4oz) soft brown sugar
1×15ml sp (1tbsp) cocoa
340ml (12fl oz) boiling water

Chocolate Fudge Dessert

1 Sift flour and cocoa together and add sugar.
2 Melt butter in a little of the milk; add remaining cold milk and vanilla essence and stir into dry ingredients. Spoon into a greased 1 litre (2pt) soufflé dish.
3 Mix together the brown sugar and 1×15ml sp (1tbsp) cocoa and sprinkle on the top.
4 Then take your courage in both hands and pour all the boiling water over the top!
5 Bake at 375°F (190°C) or in the centre of the roasting oven for 40–50 minutes. The result will be a rich chocolate pudding above a delicious chocolate sauce.

8 lamb cutlets from best end of
  neck or 450g (1lb) fillet end of
  leg of lamb
25g (1oz) seasoned flour
1×5ml sp (1tsp) fresh thyme
1×5ml sp (1tsp) fresh rosemary
2 lambs' kidneys, skinned and
  cored
450g (1lb) leeks
450g (1lb) small potatoes
salt and pepper
600ml (1pt) chicken stock
340g (12oz) frozen puff pastry
egg and milk for glazing

Welsh Lamb Pie

1 Trim the cutlets, leaving the bone in. If using leg meat, remove all the skin, fat and bone and cut into 2.5cm (1in) cubes. Coat whichever meat you are using in the seasoned flour and place in a large pie dish or roasting dish. Sprinkle with the herbs.
2 Cut each kidney into 4 slices and dip in the remaining seasoned flour. Add to the pie dish.
3 Trim the leeks and wash very carefully, cut into 2.5cm (1in) slices.
4 Peel the potatoes and cut into 1.25cm (½in) thick slices.
5 Layer the leeks and potatoes on top of the meat in the dish, season well and pour in the stock.
6 Cover the dish with foil and bake at 350°F (180°C) on the grid shelf on the bottom of the roasting oven, or in the centre of the baking oven, for 1½–2 hours. Alternatively, cook more slowly in the simmering oven for 3–4 hours.
7 Remove the dish from the oven and allow to cool for 30 minutes before putting on the pastry lid. Alternatively, cook the filling the day before or overnight in the simmering oven.
8 Roll out the thawed pastry to about 5mm (¼in) thickness and roughly 2cm (¾in) larger all round than the diameter of the top of the dish. Cut out a lid.
9 Moisten the rim of the dish and use the pastry trimmings to line the rim. Brush with water and place the lid on the top. Gently press the edges together and trim off any excess pastry with a sharp knife. Knock up and scallop the edge. Any pastry left over may be used to decorate the top of the pie, eg with leaves.
10 Glaze the top of the pie with egg mixed with a little milk and bake at 425°F (220°C) or near the top of the roasting oven for 20–30 minutes. Serve hot.

–73–
Lamb shrewsbury
Parsnip croquettes
Chocolate fudge dessert

–74–
Welsh lamb pie
Herby carrots
Banana and hazelnut fool

–75–
Mackerel with mustard sauce
Baked tomatoes
Apricot and cheese flan

Herby Carrots

1 Trim and scrub the carrots — scrape if necessary. Slice into thin sticks.
2 Place in a saucepan with the remaining ingredients and sufficient water to just cover and cook gently for 10 minutes. Alternatively, place all the ingredients in a covered ovenproof dish and bake at 350°F (180°C) on the grid shelf on the bottom of the roasting oven for 20 minutes.

450g (1lb) carrots
4×15ml sp (4tbsp) unsweetened orange juice
2×15ml sp (2tbsp) fresh chopped parsley
1×5ml sp (1tsp) fresh chopped mint
salt and pepper

Banana and Hazelnut Fool

1 Mash the bananas and brown sugar together until smooth. Combine with the yoghurt.
2 In a cup or small bowl, sprinkle the gelatine over the water; place cup in a pan of hot water to come halfway up the side and leave until dissolved.
3 Add dissolved gelatine to banana mixture.
4 Whisk the egg white until stiff but not dry and fold into the banana mixture.
5 Spoon into individual glasses, cover and chill in the refrigerator. Serve decorated with whole toasted hazelnuts.

340g (12oz) bananas (approximately 3–4)
25g (1oz) soft brown sugar
1×150g (5oz) carton hazelnut yoghurt
1×5ml sp (1tsp) powdered gelatine
2×15ml sp (2tbsp) water
1 egg white
whole toasted hazelnuts for decoration

Mackerel with Mustard Sauce

1 Clean the fish and remove the heads (or ask your fishmonger to do it for you).
2 Place the fish in an ovenproof dish and sprinkle over the celery, onions, garlic, mushrooms and parsley. Pour over the cider, cover with foil and bake at 375°F (190°C) or in the centre of the roasting oven for 20 minutes. Remove from oven and drain off the juices.
3 Gently heat together the soured cream and mustard in a pan until they are well mixed, then gradually add the stock from the fish until a thickened sauce is obtained. Pour over the fish and serve at once.

1 large or 2 medium mackerel
2 sticks celery, washed and sliced
1 bunch spring onions, chopped
1 clove garlic, crushed
110g (4oz) button mushrooms, sliced
1×15ml sp (1tbsp) fresh chopped parsley
300ml (½pt) cider
150g (¼pt) soured cream
1×15ml sp (1tbsp) dijon mustard

Baked Tomatoes

1 Halve the tomatoes, flick out the seeds, season the halves and place in a shallow ovenproof dish.
2 Chop the spring onions very finely and scatter over the tomatoes.
3 Mix together the cheese and crumbs and cover each tomato half with the mixture.
4 Spoon a little melted butter over each tomato and bake at 375°F (190°C) or in the centre of the roasting oven for 10 minutes.

450g (1lb) tomatoes
salt and pepper
4 spring onions
75g (3oz) grated cheese
3×15ml sp (3tbsp) breadcrumbs
40g (1½oz) melted butter

225g (8oz) digestive biscuits,
  crushed
110g (4oz) butter, melted
175g (6oz) low-fat curd cheese
50g (2oz) caster sugar
2 eggs
110g (4oz) ground almonds
175g (6oz) caerphilly cheese,
  grated
1 × 411g (14½oz) can apricot
  halves in natural juice
3 × 15ml sp (3tbsp) apricot juice
50g (2oz) flaked almonds

Apricot and Cheese Flan

1   Mix together the biscuit crumbs and melted butter and press into the
    base and sides of a greased deep 23cm (9in) loose-bottomed flan tin;
    chill.

2   Mix together the curd cheese and sugar until smooth. Add the eggs,
    ground almonds, caerphilly cheese and apricot juice and mix well.

3   Roughly chop the apricots and arrange in the base of the biscuit case,
    pour over the cheese mixture and scatter over the flaked almonds.

4   Bake at 325°F (160°C) or on the grid shelf on the base of the roasting
    oven with the cold plain shelf on the top set of runners, for 50–60
    minutes. For the 4-oven Aga bake on the lowest set of runners in the
    baking oven for 50–60 minutes. The flan should be pale golden and
    just set. Serve warm or cold.

Variation:
For an alternative topping, omit the flaked almonds and, when the flan is
cold, decorate with more apricot halves.

Dinner Parties

Marinated Mushrooms

1 Heat the oil in a large pan, add the streaky bacon and fry until the fat runs.
2 Add the garlic and mushrooms and cook for a further 3–4 minutes, shaking the pan and stirring the mushrooms round all the time.
3 Sprinkle on the cayenne pepper and pour over the red wine, transfer to the boiling plate and boil for a few minutes to reduce a little. Return to the simmering plate for a further 5 minutes.
4 Adjust seasoning and pour the mushrooms and wine sauce into a serving dish. Chill thoroughly before serving on lettuce leaves garnished with chopped parsley.

2 × 15ml sp (2tbsp) vegetable oil
6 rashers streaky bacon, rinded
2 cloves garlic, crushed
225g (8oz) small button mushrooms
pinch cayenne pepper
225ml (8fl oz) red wine
salt and pepper

To garnish:
lettuce leaves
2 × 15ml sp (2tbsp) fresh chopped parsley

Pot-roast Pheasant with Port *colour page 79*

1 Tie three rashers of bacon across the breast of each pheasant.
2 Heat the butter and oil together in a large flameproof casserole with a tight-fitting lid and fry the pheasants until lightly browned on all sides.
3 Cut a small cross in the base of each shallot to prevent the centre bursting out during cooking, and place in the casserole with the birds.
4 Pour over the port and stock and season if necessary. Cover tightly and bake at 350°F (180°C), in the baking oven or on the grid shelf on the base of the roasting oven for 1½ hours or until just tender.
5 Remove the pheasants and discard the bacon. Transfer the birds to a warm serving dish and surround with the onions.   (cont)

2 pheasants, prepared by the butcher and trussed
6 rashers streaky bacon, derinded
25g (1oz) butter
2 × 15ml sp (2tbsp) vegetable oil
110g (4oz) shallots or baby onions, skinned
3 × 15ml sp (3tbsp) port
150–300ml (¼–½pt) game or poultry stock
seasoning

Pot-roast Pheasant with Port –
page 77, Duchesse Potatoes
(Photography 2000)

6   Taste the cooking liquid and adjust seasoning if necessary before serving separately. Accompany this dish with Duchesse potatoes and Brussels sprouts.

Note: If the gravy is too thin, whisk in some beurre manie to thicken. Blend together equal quantities of butter and flour – about 15g (½oz) of each to 300ml (½pt) of liquid – and add in small pieces to the cooking liquid, whisking continuously until the desired thickness is reached.

450g (1lb) potatoes
50g (2oz) butter
1 egg
salt and pepper
pinch grated nutmeg

Duchesse Potatoes *colour opposite*

1   Boil potatoes in salted water, drain.
2   Sieve, mash or process the potatoes, add the butter, egg and seasonings and beat well or process until the mixture is very smooth.
3   Pipe rosettes onto a greased baking sheet using a large star nozzle. Bake at 400°F (200°C) near the top of the roasting oven for about 25 minutes or until golden brown.

900g (1½lb) victoria plums
225g (8oz) packet white almond
  paste, chilled
1×5ml sp (1tsp) cinnamon
75g (3oz) butter
8 sheets filo pastry (see page 21)
75g (3oz) flaked almonds
icing sugar to dust

Plum and Almond Strudel

1   Halve, stone and slice the plums.
2   Coarsely grate the almond paste (or whizz quickly in a food processor) and mix with the cinnamon.
3   Melt the butter.
4   Place a sheet of the pastry on a lightly floured clean tea towel and brush evenly with some of the melted butter. Place 7 more sheets on top, brushing each layer with melted butter.
5   Spread the plums over half the pastry, sprinkle with the almond mixture and 50g (2oz) of the flaked almonds.
6   With the help of the tea towel, loosely roll up the strudel, starting at the end spread with the filling. Carefully transfer to a baking sheet and seal the ends.
7   Brush with the remaining butter and sprinkle with the remaining flaked almonds. Bake at 400°F (200°C) or near the top of the roasting oven for 25–30 minutes. Serve hot dusted with icing sugar.

–77–
Marinated mushrooms
Pot-roast pheasant with port
Duchesse potatoes
Plum and almond strudel

–80–
Carrot and orange soup
Steak and pigeon pie
Cauliflower with coriander
Brandied nectarines

2 × 15ml sp (2tbsp) vegetable oil
1 onion, peeled and chopped
900g (2lb) carrots, scrubbed and
  chopped
1 × 2.5ml sp (½tsp) paprika
3 × 15ml sp (3tbsp) freshly
  chopped parsley
2 oranges, rind and juice
salt and pepper
1.2 litre (2pt) light vegetable
  stock

To garnish:
sprigs of parsley
orange slices

Carrot and Orange Soup

1   Heat the oil in a large pan, add the onion and carrots; cover the pan
    and sweat for 10 minutes over a gentle heat.
2   Add the paprika, chopped parsley, orange rind and juice, salt and pep-
    per and finally the stock; bring to the boil and simmer for 40 minutes.
    Alternatively, place in the simmering oven for 1–1½ hours or until
    the vegetables have softened. Allow to cool.
3   Liquidise, process or rub through a sieve until the soup is completely
    smooth. Adjust seasoning, then return to a clean pan and reheat gently.
    Serve garnished with parsley sprigs and thin slices of orange.

2 pigeons, breast meat only
25g (1oz) butter
450g (1lb) shin of beef, cut into
  cubes
600ml (1pt) chicken stock
salt and pepper
110g (4oz) mushrooms, sliced
1 × 1.25ml sp (¼tsp) thyme
1 × 15ml sp (1tbsp) chopped
  parsley
225g (8oz) frozen puff pastry,
  thawed
beaten egg to glaze

Steak and Pigeon Pie

1   Remove the breast meat from the pigeons – use the remainder of the
    carcase to make stock unless you have to pluck the birds yourself, in
    which case only pluck the breast and discard the rest of the carcase.
2   Brown the breasts in the butter in a flameproof casserole. Remove and
    brown the beef. Add back the pigeon plus the stock, salt and pepper,
    mushrooms and herbs. Cover and cook in the simmering oven at 300°F
    (150°C) for 2–3 hours or until all the meat is tender. Allow to cool.
3   Place a pie funnel in the middle of a 22.5cm (9in) long pie dish then
    fill dish with the cooked meats, reserving any excess gravy to serve
    separately.
4   Roll out the pastry to an oblong about 7.5cm (3in) wider and 10cm
    (4in) longer than the pie dish. Cut off extra pastry and use these strips
    to fit round the dampened rim of the dish and to make decorations for
    the lid, eg leaves and a thistle or a rose.
5   Brush the pastry-edged rim with a little water and carefully fit the
    pastry lid over the top, taking care not to stretch it. Press the two
    layers of pastry on the rim very firmly together to seal, then trim off
    any excess. Scallop the edges of the pastry.
6   Brush with beaten egg and decorate with the pastry leaves etc. Glaze
    these too. Make a hole in the pastry above the funnel.
7   Bake at 425°F (220°C) at the top of the roasting oven for 20–25 minutes
    or until the pastry is golden brown. Serve hot with the reserved gravy.

1 cauliflower
50g (2oz) butter
3 × 15ml sp (3tbsp) flour
4 × 15ml sp (4tbsp) fresh chopped
  coriander
2 × 15ml sp (2tbsp) milk or single
  cream

Cauliflower with Coriander

1   Cut the cauliflower into florets and cook in lightly salted boiling water
    until just tender. Drain and reserve cooking liquid. Place the cauli-
    flower in a shallow ovenproof dish and keep warm in the simmering
    oven.
2   Place the butter, flour and 450ml (¾pt) of the cooking liquid in a
    pan and bring to the boil, stirring constantly. Cook 1 minute.
3   Stir in the chopped coriander and milk or cream and pour over the
    cauliflower so that it is completely coated.
4   Place near the top of the roasting oven and grill until golden.

Brandied Nectarines

4 ripe nectarines or peaches
4 cloves
300ml (½pt) water
175g (6oz) granulated sugar
5cm (2in) piece of cinnamon stick
or 1×2.5ml sp (½tsp) ground
cinnamon
1×1.25ml sp (¼tsp) ground
mace
100ml (4fl oz) brandy

1 Put the nectarines in boiling water for 2–3 minutes; drain and peel carefully. Stick a clove in each one.
2 Put the water, sugar, cinnamon stick and mace in a deep pan and dissolve the sugar slowly.
3 Put the nectarines in the syrup and cook them gently for 15–20 minutes, making sure they are completely covered by the syrup. This cooking ensures the nectarines will not discolour when stored.
4 Carefully lift the nectarines into a wide-mouthed, screw-topped jar. Remove the cinnamon stick from the syrup and stir in the brandy. Pour over the nectarines and leave to cool slightly before covering tightly. Stand in a cool place and keep for 3 days before using by which time the brandied syrup will have fully penetrated the fruit. If you want to keep these nectarines longer, double the amount of brandy.

Cucumber with Prawns and Yoghurt

1 cucumber
110g (4oz) button mushrooms
25g (1oz) butter
1×5ml sp (1tsp) plain flour
65ml (2½fl oz) chicken stock
65ml (2½fl oz) natural yoghurt
salt and pepper
few drops soy sauce
175g (6oz) shelled prawns

To garnish:
lemon twists
prawns in shells
finely chopped fresh basil

1 Wash the cucumber and cut into small dice. Cook for 3–4 minutes in boiling salted water. Rinse in cold water and drain thoroughly.
2 Trim the mushrooms but leave whole unless they are very large in which case slice into thick slices.
3 Melt the butter in a pan and cook the mushrooms for 2–3 minutes. Add the cucumber and simmer, covered, for a further 2–3 minutes.
4 Sprinkle in the flour and blend thoroughly before gradually adding the stock and then the yoghurt, stirring until smooth. Season and add the soy sauce and cook for a further 1 minute.
5 Stir in the shelled prawns and spoon into warmed ramekin dishes. Sprinkle with the basil and garnish each with a twist of lemon and a whole prawn. Serve hot with brown bread and butter.

Chicken and Spinach Strudels

1 bunch spring onions, chopped
1 clove garlic, crushed
1×15ml sp (1tbsp) vegetable oil
450g (1lb) spinach, fresh or frozen
175g (6oz) feta cheese, crumbled
1×150ml (5fl oz) tub greek
yoghurt
200g (7oz) cooked chicken, finely
diced
6 sheets filo pastry, about 225g
(8oz) (see page 21)
75g (3oz) butter, melted
1×15ml sp (1tbsp) sesame seeds

1 Gently fry the onions and garlic in the vegetable oil.
2 If using fresh spinach, wash and drain and cook in a large pan with a very little water for 8–10 minutes. If using frozen spinach, cook gently until thawed. Drain well and chop.
3 Mix together the cooked spinach, onions, garlic, feta cheese, yoghurt and chicken.
4 Cut each sheet of pastry in half across the width using scissors. Brush one piece with melted butter and place a little of the filling along the longer edge. Roll up into a long sausage and roll each end towards the centre to seal. Repeat with the remaining 11 sheets.
5 Place the strudels on a greased baking sheet and brush with melted butter. Sprinkle with the sesame seeds and bake at 400°F (200°C) or in the centre of the roasting oven for 20–30 minutes. Serve with boiled and buttered baby sweetcorn.

Chicken Liver Pâté – page 85
(Kenwood)

225g (8oz) butter
75g (3oz) light soft brown sugar
225g (8oz) plain flour
75g (3oz) walnuts, chopped
225g (8oz) fresh blackberries
300ml (½pt) double cream,
  whipped

Blackberry Shortcake

1   Beat the butter until light and fluffy, then beat in the sugar. Stir in the flour until well mixed, followed by the chopped walnuts. Mix to a firm dough, then turn onto a floured surface and knead lightly.
2   Divide the dough in half and roll each piece into a 20cm (8in) circle. Place on greased baking sheets. If the mixture is rather soft roll out directly on the baking sheets. Prick all over with a fork and mark the top of one shortcake round into 8 sections without cutting right through. Chill for 30 minutes.
3   Bake at 400°F (200°C) in the centre of the roasting oven for about 20 minutes or until firm to the touch and golden brown. Cut through the marked divisions on the one shortcake round and leave to cool on the baking trays.
4   Set aside 8 blackberries for decoration. Mix the remainder with two-thirds of the cream and spread over the plain round shortcake.
5   Place the sectioned shortcake on the top; pipe a whirl of cream on each section and top with a blackberry.

450g (1lb) onions
50g (2oz) butter
1 litre (2pt) beef stock
salt and pepper
25g (1oz) plain flour
4 slices french bread 1.25cm
  (½in) thick
50g (2oz) grated cheese
  eg gruyère

–81–
Cucumber with prawns and
yoghurt
Chicken and spinach strudels
Baby sweetcorn
Blackberry shortcake

–82–
French onion soup
Mediterranean red mullet
Buttered courgettes
Gâteau mille feuilles

French Onion Soup *colour page 71*

1   Peel and thinly slice the onions.
2   Melt 25g (1oz) of the butter in a large pan and add the onions. Cover and cook on the simmering plate for 10–15 minutes until the onions are soft and transparent.
3   Remove the lid and continue frying the onions until they are golden brown.
4   Stir in the stock and seasoning, replace the lid and continue to simmer for 30 minutes.
5   Mix the flour with a little of the hot soup and return to the pan, bring to the boil and simmer for 2–3 minutes.
6   Meanwhile, butter both sides of the bread and place on a baking sheet, sprinkle over the grated cheese and bake on the grid shelf on the base of the roasting oven 350°F (180°C) for 5–10 minutes or until the bread is crisp and the cheese melted.
7   Place a slice of bread in each soup bowl and pour over the hot onion soup. Serve immediately.

4 tomatoes
1 green pepper, seeded and sliced
1 yellow pepper, seeded and sliced
1 clove garlic, crushed
110g (4oz) button mushrooms
salt and pepper
4 red mullet
300ml (½pt) red wine
fresh chopped basil or marjoram

Mediterranean Red Mullet

1 Skin tomatoes by plunging into boiling water for 1 minute. Cut into quarters and remove seeds. Place in a large ovenproof dish with the peppers, crushed garlic and button mushrooms (slice if they are large). Season.
2 Clean the red mullet and wash in cold water. Place side by side on top of the vegetables and pour over the wine.
3 Cover tightly with foil and bake at 375°F (190°C), on the grid shelf on the base of the roasting oven for 25–30 minutes or until the fish flake easily. Serve garnished with freshly chopped basil or marjoram.

450g (1lb) courgettes
25g (1oz) butter
1×15ml sp (1tbsp) water
salt and pepper
1×15ml sp (1tbsp) fresh chopped
  parsley
1×15ml sp (1tbsp) fresh chopped
  mixed herbs

Buttered Courgettes

1 Wipe and trim courgettes and place in a flameproof casserole or dish with the butter and water. Season and cover tightly to conserve all the juices.
2 Cook at the bottom of the roasting oven on the grid shelf at 350–375°F (180–190°C) for 20–30 minutes or until tender.
3 Sprinkle with the parsley and mixed herbs and serve hot.

1×398g (13oz) packet frozen puff
  pastry, thawed

Filling:
175g (6oz) full fat soft cheese
50g (2oz) caster sugar
150ml (¼pt) double cream,
  lightly whipped
225g (8oz) fresh strawberries

Topping:
110g (4oz) icing sugar, sifted
3×15ml sp (3tbsp) redcurrant
  jelly

Gâteau Mille Feuilles

1 Roll out pastry quite thinly and cut into two rectangles each 20×7.5cm (8×3in). Place on greased baking sheets and prick at regular intervals. Leave to rest for 30 minutes in the refrigerator.
2 Bake the pastry at 400°F (200°C) or near the top of the roasting oven for 15–20 minutes or until lightly golden and well risen. Allow to cool.
3 Soften the cheese in a bowl and beat in the caster sugar. Fold in the lightly whipped cream.
4 Hull the strawberries and cut any large ones in half. Arrange over one baked pastry strip. Cover with the cream cheese mixture. Place the second pastry strip on top.
5 Mix the icing sugar with a little hot water to give a thin coating icing and spread evenly over the top pastry strip.
6 Place the redcurrant jelly in a piping bag fitted with a No 3 plain piping nozzle and pipe parallel lines over the icing at 1.25cm (½in) intervals. Alternatively, warm the jelly and use a teaspoon to drizzle lines across the icing. Take a skewer and drag it across the jelly lines from right to left and then left to right in alternate lines to give a feathered effect. Allow to set.

Note: Do not assemble this dessert too far in advance as the pastry will lose its crispness.

Chicken Liver Pâté *colour page 83*

1   Chop onion and garlic finely and soften in 25g (1oz) butter until just turning colour.
2   Add the livers, bouquet garni and seasoning and fry together for about 3 minutes. Cool.
3   Melt remaining butter, add to the cooked mixture and liquidise or process until very smooth.
4   Add the brandy then pour into a china pot or 4 ramekin dishes, smooth over the top and cover with a layer of clarified butter. Cover and chill. Serve with hot toast. For a more elaborate presentation, line the china pot with cooked rashers of bacon. When chilled, turn out onto a serving plate and garnish with sliced stuffed olives and sliced gherkins.

Note: To clarify butter; melt the butter, leave to settle, then strain through muslin.
This pâté is best made in advance to allow the flavour to mature. It freezes very well.

1 medium onion
1 clove garlic
110g (4oz) butter
225g (8oz) chicken livers
1 small bouquet garni
salt and pepper
1 × 15ml sp (1tbsp) brandy
50–75g (2–3oz) unsalted butter, clarified
4 rashers streaky bacon (optional)
stuffed olives (optional)
small gherkins (optional)

Mulled Beef Casserole (Cadbury Schweppes)

300ml (½pt) red wine
2 cinnamon sticks
6 juniper berries
450g (1lb) chuck or braising steak
1 large onion, sliced
110g (4oz) streaky bacon, rinded and chopped
vegetable oil
2×15ml sp (2tbsp) flour
300ml (½pt) beef stock
salt and pepper
4 lambs' kidneys
110g (4oz) small button mushrooms
1 green pepper, sliced
1 yellow pepper, sliced

Mulled Beef Casserole *colour above*

1   Pour the wine into a saucepan, add the cinnamon sticks and the crushed juniper berries. Bring to the boil, remove from the heat and cool.
2   Cut the meat into bite-sized pieces. Place the meat and onions in a bowl and pour over the cold wine. Cover and refrigerate overnight. Next day, drain the meat and onions, reserving the marinade.
3   In a large flameproof casserole, fry the bacon in its own fat, drain and remove.
4   Adding a little oil if necessary fry the marinaded meat. Add back the bacon and onions and sprinkle in the flour; cook for 1 minute. Pour in the stock and reserved marinade and season. Bring to the boil, cover and cook at 300°F (150°C) in the simmering oven for 3–4 hours or until the meat is almost tender.
5   Halve the kidneys, snip out the core and peel away any membrane; cut into bite-sized pieces. Wipe the mushrooms. Stir the kidneys, mushrooms and sliced peppers into the casserole, bring back to the boil and return to the oven for a further hour. Alternatively, place on the grid shelf on the bottom of the roasting oven at 350–375°F (180–190°C) for a further 20 minutes. Serve hot.

Potato and Carrot Bake

900g (2lb) potatoes
675g (1½lb) carrots
25g (1oz) butter
2 eggs, separated
salt and pepper
2×15ml sp (2tbsp) coarse oatmeal

1   Peel the potatoes and scrub the carrots; cut both into similar sized pieces. Cook together in boiling salted water for 15–20 minutes or until tender. Drain well.

2   Mash or process the vegetables, beat in the butter and egg yolks; season.

3   Whisk the egg whites until stiff but not dry and fold into the vegetable purée.

4   Spoon into a lightly greased shallow ovenproof dish and sprinkle with the oatmeal. Bake at 400°F (200°C) in the centre of the roasting oven for 25–30 minutes until well risen and golden brown.

Salambos

75g (3oz) butter
225ml (8fl oz) water
100g (3¾oz) plain flour
pinch salt
3 eggs

Caramel topping:
125g (5oz) caster sugar
1×15ml sp (1tbsp) water

Orange cream:
1 orange
1×15ml sp (1tbsp) icing sugar
300ml (½pt) double cream

1   Prepare choux pastry by melting the butter in the water, then bring to the boil and remove from the heat immediately. Beat in the sifted flour and salt using a wooden spoon. Stir over a low heat until the pastry comes together and forms a soft ball. Cool slightly. Beat in the eggs one at a time, beating well with a wooden spoon until each egg is completely absorbed The mixture will be very smooth and shiny and just hold its shape (if large eggs are used you may not need to use all of them).

2   Either pipe mixture in bun shapes onto baking trays using a 1.25cm (½in) diameter plain nozzle or put small spoonfuls of the mixture onto trays. Bake at 425°F (220°C) near the top of the roasting oven for 10 minutes. Then lower the trays to the base of the oven or place in the baking oven at 350–375°F (180–190°C), for a further 20 minutes or until golden. Make a slit in the side of each bun to release the steam and leave to cool on a wire rack.

3   Prepare caramel topping by putting the caster sugar and water into a small, heavy-based pan and dissolving over a low heat. Transfer to the boiling plate and boil until the caramel is a rich brown colour; be careful not to overcook it or it will burn. Stop the caramel cooking by dipping the bottom of the pan in warm water.

4   When the caramel is ready, dip the top of each choux bun into it and leave to cool on a rack.

5   Using a zester, remove the zest from the orange; mix with a little of the orange juice and the icing sugar.

6   Whip the cream and carefully fold in the orange mixture; do not make the cream too thick or it will curdle when you add the orange. Make a slit in the side of each choux bun and fill with the cream.

-85-
Chicken liver pâté
Mulled beef casserole
Potato and carrot bake
Salambos

-88-
Soufflé stuffed tomatoes
Hungarian pork
Stir-fried cabbage with walnuts
Chocolate roulade

-90-
Prawn stuffed eggs with
asparagus
Stuffed pork en croûte
Potato boulangère
Baked beetroot with orange
Bavarian cream

4 large beef tomatoes (or 12
  smaller ones)
50ml (2fl oz) milk
110g (4oz) blue shropshire cheese,
  grated
1 clove garlic, crushed
2 eggs, separated
salt and pepper

Soufflé Stuffed Tomatoes

1 Cut a lid from the base of each tomato and keep to one side. Scoop out the seeds and flesh carefully with a spoon. Lightly salt the insides of the tomatoes and drain them, upside down on a plate, for about 15 minutes.

2 Heat the milk gently in a pan until lukewarm. Add 75g (3oz) of the cheese, the crushed garlic, 2 egg yolks and seasoning. Continue to heat gently, stirring continuously, until the cheese melts and the mixture thickens slightly. If the heat is too fierce, this process can be done in a double boiler or in a bowl over a pan of simmering water.

3 In a separate bowl whisk the egg white until just stiff; fold into the cheese mixture.

4 Divide the soufflé mixture between the tomato shells and place in a lightly oiled ovenproof dish. Sprinkle with the remaining cheese and top with the lids. Bake at 375°F (190°C) on the grid shelf at the bottom of the roasting oven for about 20 minutes or until the soufflé mixture is set. Serve immediately.

700g (1½lb) pork fillet or
  boned leg of pork
2×15ml sp (2tbsp) vegetable oil
1 large onion, sliced
2 cloves garlic, crushed
4×5ml sp (4tsp) paprika
1.25ml sp (¼tsp) caraway seeds
1.25ml sp (¼tsp) cayenne pepper
generous pinch marjoram and
  thyme
1 bay leaf
salt and pepper
2 red peppers, seeded and sliced
1 yellow pepper, seeded and sliced
225g (8oz) button mushrooms
1×397g (14oz) can tomatoes
300ml (½pt) stock

To garnish:
paprika
chopped fresh parsley
150ml (¼pt) soured cream

Hungarian Pork

1 Cut the meat into bite-sized pieces, sauté in the oil in a flameproof casserole. Lift out and keep warm.

2 Sauté the onion and garlic in the oil until soft. Add the spices and seasonings and cook for a further 2–3 minutes.

3 Add the peppers and mushrooms (slice mushrooms if large) and cook for 2 minutes.

4 Add back the pork and then pour over the chopped tomatoes, juice and stock; stir and bring to the boil. Cover the casserole and cook in the simmering oven at 250°F (130°C) for 2–3 hours or until the meat is tender.

5 Dust with paprika and parsley and serve with soured cream swirled on the top.

Stir-fried Cabbage with Walnuts

700g (1½lb) green winter cabbage
450g (1lb) carrots
3×15ml sp (3tbsp) vegetable oil
1 lemon, rind and juice
2×5ml sp (2tsp) soy sauce
3×15ml sp (3tbsp) stock
50g (2oz) walnuts
salt and pepper

1 Shred the cabbage into large pieces, discarding any coarse outer leaves. Wash and drain well. Scrub the carrots and cut into thin flat strips.

2 Heat the oil in a large frying pan or wok and cook the carrots, stirring continuously, for 2–3 minutes or until they begin to soften.

3 Mix in the cabbage, grated lemon rind and juice, soy sauce and stock. Cook, stirring, for a further 2–3 minutes or until the cabbage is just cooked.

4 Add the walnuts and season. Serve immediately.

Chocolate Roulade

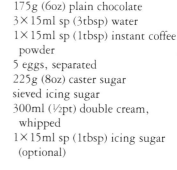

175g (6oz) plain chocolate
3×15ml sp (3tbsp) water
1×15ml sp (1tbsp) instant coffee powder
5 eggs, separated
225g (8oz) caster sugar
sieved icing sugar
300ml (½pt) double cream, whipped
1×15ml sp (1tbsp) icing sugar (optional)

1 Place the chocolate, water and coffee powder in a bowl over a pan of boiling water and heat gently until the chocolate has melted. Beat with a fork until smooth and leave to cool slightly.

2 Beat the egg yolks with the caster sugar until thick and creamy, then fold in the warm chocolate mixture.

3 Whisk the egg whites until stiff and fold into the chocolate mixture. Turn into a greased and lined 20×30cm (8×12in) swiss roll tin (use silicon paper or greased greaseproof paper). Bake at 350°F (180°C) in the centre of the baking oven, or on the grid shelf on the bottom of the roasting oven protected by the cold solid shelf, for 20–25 minutes or until firm to the touch.

4 Leave to cool in the tin for 5 minutes (it will crack and sink slightly), then cover with a piece of dampened greaseproof paper and a clean damp tea towel. Leave in the refrigerator overnight to set.

5 Carefully remove the tea towel and greaseproof paper and turn the roulade out onto a piece of silicon or greaseproof paper thickly sprinkled with sieved icing sugar. Peel off the lining paper very carefully.

6 Sweeten the cream with 1×15ml sp (1tbsp) of icing sugar if liked, then spread over the roulade and roll up like a Swiss roll. It will probably crack in places. Transfer to a serving plate.

Note: This dessert can successfully be frozen once completed but it does not freeze solid so should be kept in a rigid container to protect it from damage.

4 eggs
40g (1½oz) softened butter
1×2.5ml sp (½tsp) paprika
  pepper
225g (8oz) shelled prawns
salt and pepper
340g (12oz) frozen or tinned
  asparagus
300ml (½pt) milk
25g (1oz) plain flour
25g (1oz) butter
25g (1oz) freshly grated parmesan
  cheese

Prawn Stuffed Eggs with Asparagus

1 Hard boil the eggs, shell and cut in half lengthways. Sieve the yolks and place the whites in a bowl of cold water.
2 Cream together the butter and paprika and mix with the sieved yolks. Add 75g (3oz) of the prawns, finely chopped. Season to taste.
3 If using frozen asparagus, cook according to instructions on packet, drain and refresh with cold water to set the colour, drain again. Divide asparagus between 4 shallow ovenproof dishes.
4 Make the sauce by placing the milk, flour and butter in a pan over a gentle heat and stirring until it thickens; continue cooking for a further minute. Season.
5 Drain the egg whites and fill with the prawn mixture and place on the asparagus. Scatter the remaining whole prawns on the top and coat with the sauce. Sprinkle with the cheese and bake at 400°F (200°C) in the centre of the roasting oven for 15–20 minutes. Serve hot.

1 pork tenderloin weighing about
  450g (1lb)
1 medium onion, finely chopped
2×15ml sp (2tbsp) vegetable oil
1×2.5ml sp (½tsp) thyme
1×2.5ml sp (½tsp) sage
1×5ml sp (1tsp) freshly chopped
  parsley
110g (4oz) mushrooms, finely
  chopped
110g (4oz) breadcrumbs
1 orange, grated rind and juice
1 egg
salt and pepper
225g (8oz) streaky bacon rashers,
  rinded
225g (8oz) frozen puff pastry,
  defrosted
beaten egg to glaze
1×5ml sp (1tsp) flour
300ml (½pt) red wine or good
  stock
watercress

Stuffed Pork en Croûte

1 With a sharp knife, split the tenderloin in half lengthways and, using a rolling pin, batter the two halves to flatten and widen them.
2 Soften the onion in the oil with the herbs, then add the mushrooms and cook for a further 3–4 minutes or until the juices from the mushrooms have almost evaporated.
3 Empty the contents of the pan into a bowl and add the breadcrumbs, orange rind, egg and sufficient orange juice to bind the stuffing. Season.
4 Spoon the stuffing onto one half of the tenderloin, patting it down firmly, place the other half on top.
5 Lay the bacon rashers out, overlapping slightly, to a rectangle the length of the meat. Place the meat in the middle and wrap in the bacon. Hold bacon in place with cocktail sticks then neatly tie at intervals — remove cocktail sticks before cooking.
6 Carefully transfer to a roasting tin and bake at 400°F (200°C) in the centre of the roasting oven for 1 hour, basting frequently. Leave until quite cold and reserve pan juices.
7 Roll out pastry to a rectangle sufficient to completely cover the cooked pork. Trim the edges (keep the trimmings for decoration) and turn the pastry over so that the rolled surface, the best side of the pastry, is on the outside when baked.
8 Set the meat on the pastry, dampen the pastry edges and roll round the meat; tuck in the ends and press firmly.
9 Place on a baking sheet and brush all over with beaten egg. Make pastry decorations, eg crescents or leaves, and place on the top, brush with egg. Bake at 425°F (220°C) or near the top of the roasting oven for about 30 minutes or until nicely golden brown.
10 Add the flour to the pan juices and cook for 1 minute. Gradually stir in the wine or stock and cook until the gravy thickens. Season to taste.
11 Serve the pork garnished with the watercress. Serve the gravy separately.

Potato Boulangère

900g (2lb) potatoes
1 onion
salt and pepper
150ml (¼pt) white stock
150ml (¼pt) milk
50g (2oz) butter

1   Butter a large shallow ovenproof dish.
2   Peel the potatoes and cut into thin slices (use a food processor for this if you have one). Peel the onion and slice thinly.
3   Arrange a layer of potato over the bottom of the dish, followed by a layer of onion and a seasoning of salt and pepper. Continue with another layer of potatoes and so on, finishing with a layer of potato.
4   Pour over the stock and milk and fleck the top with the butter.
5   Bake at 375°F (190°C) at the bottom of the roasting oven on the grid shelf for 45–50 minutes or until the potatoes are cooked and the top layer browned. If the potatoes are cut too thickly this dish will take much longer to cook. Serve hot.

Baked Beetroot with Orange

3 raw beetroot, about 675g (1½lb)
1 large orange, grated rind and juice
salt and pepper

1   Scrub the beetroot and trim the ends but do not peel. Place in a shallow ovenproof dish, cover tightly with foil and bake at 350°F (180°C) in the baking oven, or on the grid shelf at the bottom of the roasting oven protected by the solid shelf, for 2 hours or until tender when pierced.
2   Allow to cool slightly then peel each beetroot using a knife and fork. Cut into wedges and place in a serving dish.
3   Stir the orange rind and juice into the warm beetroot, season if necessary and serve immediately.

Bavarian Cream

3 eggs, separated
50g (2oz) caster sugar
450ml (¾pt) milk
1 vanilla pod or 2–3 drops vanilla essence
1 × 15ml sp (1tbsp) instant coffee granules
4 × 5ml rounded sp (4 rounded tsp) powdered gelatine
5 × 15ml sp (5tbsp) water
150ml (¼pt) double cream
cream to decorate (optional)

1   Cream together the egg yolks and sugar until pale and creamy.
2   Put the milk into a pan with the vanilla pod and heat gently until it just reaches boiling point. Remove the vanilla pod and stir in the coffee granules until dissolved.
3   Gently pour the milk onto the yolks and blend in well. Return to the pan and stir continually over a gentle heat until the custard coats the back of the spoon. This will take about 15 minutes. Do not allow the mixture to boil or it will curdle. If the heat is too high, put the custard in a bowl over a pan of simmering water to thicken it.
4   Dissolve the gelatine in the water over a pan of simmering water. Carefully stir into the warm custard and mix thoroughly. Turn the custard into a bowl and place this in a larger bowl of ice cubes and water and stir continuously until thick but still flowing.
5   Lightly whip the cream, whisk the egg whites until stiff but not dry. Gently but thoroughly fold the cream into the coffee custard. Pour the custard onto the egg whites and fold in quickly but lightly with a metal spoon until no pockets of egg white are visible. However, do not overfold as this will beat out the air and the bavarois will be solid.
6   Pour into a lightly oiled 1.2 litre (2½pt) capacity mould and put in the refrigerator to set.
7   To serve, remove the moulded bavarois from the refrigerator and allow to stand for 15 minutes. Then carefully ease the bavarois away from the

Chicken Normandie – page 93
(Colman's)

9 Whisk the egg whites until stiff and whisk in the remaining caster sugar. Fold lightly but thoroughly into the cheese mixture, together with the crushed meringue. Spoon the mixture into the prepared tin and shake the tin gently to level the surface. Place the meringue round on the top. Chill for 3–4 hours or until set.

10 Carefully release the sides of the tin from the cheesecake and lift the cheesecake out on the tin base.

Note: If you are unable to obtain greek yoghurt or crème fraîche use soured cream.

This dessert is best made the day it is to be eaten as the crushed meringue will eventually soften and cause the cheesecake to 'weep'.

–92–
Crab stuffed avocado
Chicken normandie
Baby broad beans
Raspberry meringue cheesecake

Special Occasions

–95–
SUNDAY LUNCH
Roast ribs of beef
Roast potatoes
Parsnip balls
Braised red cabbage
Yorkshire pudding
Plum cheesecake

SUNDAY LUNCH

Roast Ribs of Beef

1 Wipe the meat and season well. Score the fat on top of the ribs both ways and rub in the dripping or oil, salt and mustard.
2 Stand the ribs upright in a dry meat tin and place as high as possible in the roasting oven for 1 hour.
3 Lower the meat tin to the lowest set of runners for a further 10 minutes per 450g (1lb), longer if you prefer the meat well done.
4 When cooked, remove the meat to a warm dish and place in the simmering or warming oven to set while you make the gravy.
5 For the gravy: place the roasting tin on the simmering plate and fry the residues until brown. Add the flour and cook for a further minute. Gradually add the water and wine, and boil rapidly for 2 minutes. Check the seasoning and strain into a small pan. Skim off any surface fat, reheat and serve.

2–3 ribs of beef
salt and pepper
2 × 15ml sp (2tbsp) beef dripping
  or vegetable oil
1 × 5ml sp (1tsp) salt
2 × 5ml sp (2tsp) dry mustard
  (optional)
1–2 × 15ml sp (1–2tbsp) flour
450–600ml (¾–1pt) water
  (preferably vegetable water)
150ml (¼pt) red wine (optional)

Roast Potatoes

Peel potatoes and par-boil in salted water for 5 minutes on the simmering plate. Either roast round the meat in the meat juices for 1 hour, basting once, or place in a dish of hot fat and cook above the meat, again for about 1 hour.

675g (1½lb) parsnips, peeled
  and cut into 2.5cm (1in) cubes
75g (3oz) butter
2×15ml sp (2tbsp) double cream
salt and pepper
1×1.25ml sp (¼tsp) freshly
  grated nutmeg
½ egg, beaten
50g (2oz) dried breadcrumbs
oil for frying
chopped parsley for sprinkling

Parsnip Balls

1 Put the parsnips in a pan of cold salted water, cover and bring to the boil. Cook for 15 minutes or until tender. Drain thoroughly.
2 Melt the butter in a pan on the simmering plate and add it to the parsnips with the cream, salt and pepper and nutmeg; mash well. Allow to cool, then stir in the egg.
3 Using your fingers, form the mixture into walnut-sized balls and roll in the breadcrumbs.
4 Put the oil into a deep pan and heat on the boiling plate to 400°F (200°F).
5 In a frying basket, place as many balls as will fit without touching. Lower the basket carefully into the hot oil and fry for 2–3 minutes until golden brown. Repeat with batches of balls until they are all cooked, keeping them warm in either the simmering or the warming oven.
6 Serve hot sprinkled with chopped parsley.

Variation:
Parsnip balls are also delicious covered with cheese sauce and browned in the oven, and served with a salad for a light lunch.

Note: Transfer the pan of oil to the simmering plate if necessary to prevent the fat getting too hot.

900g (2lb) red cabbage
1×15ml sp (1tbsp) oil
2 onions, peeled and sliced into
  rings
2 cooking apples, peeled and
  sliced
1×2.5ml sp (½tsp) whole
  caraway seeds (optional)
75ml (3fl oz) red wine or red wine
  vinegar
salt and pepper

Braised Red Cabbage

1 Remove any tough or wilted outer leaves of the cabbage, quarter, remove the core and shred finely.
2 Heat the oil in a cast-iron casserole on the simmering plate and gently fry the onion rings until soft but not coloured.
3 Add the apples and caraway seeds and stir in well.
4 Finally add the shredded cabbage and wine or vinegar, cover and cook in the simmering oven at 300°F (150°C) for 1½–2 hours. Stir from time to time and moisten with a little extra water or vinegar if necessary. Adjust seasoning and serve hot.

Note: Red cabbage is cooked in as little liquid as possible so that it is, in effect, steamed. It will then be soft without losing its texture. This dish keeps well and will reheat, so it can be made the previous day if necessary.

110g (4oz) plain flour
pinch of salt
1 egg
300ml (½pt) milk or milk and
  water mixed
dripping

Yorkshire Pudding

1 Sift the flour and salt into a bowl, break the egg into the centre and add a little of the milk. Gradually mix together and then beat well. Add sufficient of the remaining liquid to make a batter the consistency of single cream. Leave to stand for about 1 hour.
2 Heat a little dripping to smoking point in 12 deep patty tins or a pie dish standing in a half-size meat tin. Pour a little of the batter into each tin and cook at the top of the oven (if using a pie dish in a meat tin, hang on the top set of runners) for 30 minutes until crisp and risen. Serve immediately.

Plum Cheesecake

75g (3oz) butter
50g (2oz) soft brown sugar
110g (4oz) jumbo oats
1 egg yolk

1 Melt the butter and sugar together over a low heat and stir in the oats and egg yolk. Press evenly over the base of a greased loose-bottomed 18–20cm (7–8in) cake tin or spring-clip tin. Chill.
2 Reserve 4 plums for decoration. Halve and stone the remaining plums and arrange over the oaty base.
3 Soften the cheese in a large bowl and beat in the egg yolks, almond essence, 50g (2oz) of the caster sugar, the ground almonds and the whipping cream.
4 Whisk the egg whites until stiff, then whisk in the remaining caster sugar. Fold thoroughly into the cheese mixture and spoon into the prepared tin on top of the plums; smooth the surface.
5 Bake at 325°F (160°C) for 1½–1¾ hours or until firm but spongy to the touch, or at the bottom of the baking oven for the same length of time. Alternatively, begin baking at the bottom of the roasting oven on the grid shelf protected by the cold solid shelf on the top set of runners and once set remove to the top of the simmering oven for the remainder of the cooking period.
6 Once cooked, open the door of the simmering oven and leave the cheesecake placed at the bottom, to cool for about 1 hour. (This should help prevent sinking of the mixture in the centre and excessive shrinkage.)
7 Ease the sides of the tin carefully away from the cheesecake and lift out on the metal base. Spread the crème fraîche over the top and decorate with the remaining plums halved and the toasted almonds. (Toast flaked almonds by placing on a baking tray at the top of the roasting oven and grilling until golden.) Chill for 2–3 hours before serving.

Filling:
450g (1lb) ripe dessert plums
225g (8oz) curd cheese
3 eggs, separated
few drops almond essence
110g (4oz) caster sugar
25g (1oz) ground almonds
150ml (¼pt) whipping cream
150ml (¼pt) crème fraîche
25g (1oz) toasted almonds

CELEBRATION BUFFET

Crab Mousse

3 envelopes gelatine
3×200g (7oz) cans crab meat
1 small onion, grated
3×15ml sp (3tbsp) white wine vinegar
180ml (6fl oz) fish stock or water
2×450g (16oz) cartons natural yoghurt or greek yoghurt *or*
1×450g (16oz) carton natural yoghurt and 450g (16oz) mayonnaise
150g (5oz) peeled prawns
salt and pepper
watercress to garnish

1 Sprinkle the gelatine over 6×15ml sp (6tbsp) water in a saucepan and dissolve gently on the simmering plate; do not overheat. Remove from the heat and leave to cool.
2 Drain the crab and either pound or process until very smooth. Mix with the remaining ingredients (except watercress) and the cooled gelatine.
3 Lightly oil a 21.5cm (8½in) ring mould or spring clip tin with ring base and pour in the mixture. Leave to set in a cool place or refrigerator.
4 When set, turn the mousse out onto a serving dish and garnish with watercress.

340g (12oz) raw turkey, minced
450g (1lb) raw gammon, minced
450g (1lb) sausagemeat
salt and pepper
1 onion, grated
1×15ml sp (1tbsp) each fresh
  chopped parsley, rosemary and
  chives or 1×15ml sp (1tbsp)
  dried mixed herbs
2×15ml sp (2tbsp) lemon juice
3×15ml sp (3tbsp) brandy
  (optional)

Marinade mixture:
225–275g (8–10oz) raw turkey
  breast, cut into strips or 225g
  (8oz) cooked sliced ham
3×15ml sp (3tbsp) white wine
3×15ml sp (3tbsp) sunflower oil
1×15ml sp (1tbsp) chopped
  parsley

Pastry:
340g (12oz) plain flour (white or
  wholemeal)
1×5ml sp (1tsp) salt
1 egg, beaten
110g (4oz) lard
150ml (¼pt) warm water (see
  method)
4 hard-boiled eggs, shelled
beaten egg to glaze
25g (1oz) gelatine

Raised Turkey and Ham Pie

1   Mix together the turkey, gammon, sausagemeat, seasoning, onion, mixed herbs, lemon juice and brandy.
2   Marinate the turkey strips or ham overnight or for 12 hours in the wine and oil with the chopped parsley.
3   Place the flour and salt in a bowl, place the egg on one side of bowl and cover with flour. Melt the lard with 150ml (¼pt) warm water and pour on to the other side of the flour. Mix well until it forms a large ball. (If using wholemeal flour a little more warm water will be needed otherwise the pastry will be a little dry and is likely to crack when cooked.)
4   Knead the dough on a lightly floured board until smooth. Roll out two-thirds to a circle 5cm (2in) larger than the diameter of the tin – a deep 20cm (8in) loose-bottomed cake tin which has been lightly greased. Wrap remaining pastry in clingfilm and keep warm until required to prevent a crust forming.
5   Carefully line the tin with the circle of pastry, easing it into the base and pressing it evenly up the sides. Take care not to tear the pastry as the crack formed will open up during cooking and let out all the juices.
6   Place half the turkey, gammon and sausagemeat mixture in the base of the tin and cover with the marinated mixture. Place the four hard-boiled eggs on top, then cover with the remaining sausagemeat mixture. Pack down neatly and firmly.
7   Roll out the remaining pastry to fit top and cut decorative leaves out of the excess. Brush edge with the beaten egg and place lid on the top, seal edge firmly and trim. Brush top with egg, add the leaves then brush again. Make a hole in the centre.
8   Bake on a baking tray on the grid shelf on the base of the roasting oven protected by the cold solid shelf for about 1½ hours at 350°F (180°C). For a 4-oven Aga, bake in the centre of the baking oven for the same time.
9   After 1 hour, gently remove pie from the tin (the pastry should have set sufficiently to hold the pie in shape without cracking) and brush the sides with beaten egg. Return to the oven and continue cooking until golden and firm. Remove pie from the oven and cool completely.
10 Dissolve the gelatine in a little hot water on the simmering plate, then make up to 450ml (¾pt) with cold water. Leave until just beginning to set. Carefully pour into the pie through the hole in the top and leave pie in a cool place to set before cutting.

Note: Hot-water crust pastry is not difficult to make but it must be kept warm and used quickly after making to prevent it drying out. Special fluted moulds with hinged sides can be used, but a well-greased loose-bottomed cake tin does just as well. The pastry can also be moulded over a floured jar.

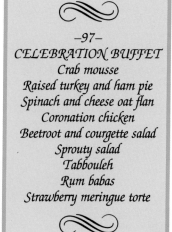

–97–
CELEBRATION BUFFET
Crab mousse
Raised turkey and ham pie
Spinach and cheese oat flan
Coronation chicken
Beetroot and courgette salad
Sprouty salad
Tabbouleh
Rum babas
Strawberry meringue torte

Spinach and Cheese Oat Flan

1 Place the flour, oatmeal, sesame seeds and salt in a mixing bowl and rub in the fats until the mixture resembles fine breadcrumbs. Add the water and mix to a firm dough.
2 Turn out onto a floured board and knead lightly until smooth. Roll out and line a 20cm (8in) deep-sided loose-bottomed fluted flan tin or a 25cm (10in) shallow-sided tin. Chill while making the filling.
3 If using fresh spinach, wash the leaves, place in a large pan on the simmering plate and cook gently for about 5 minutes, turning once or twice. Drain thoroughly and chop finely. Frozen spinach should be placed in a sieve and the liquid pressed out firmly using a potato masher or wooden spoon.
4 Heat the oil and gently cook the spring onions until just softening.
5 Mix together the spinach, onions, curd cheese, eggs, cheddar cheese and milk. Season and add a pinch of grated nutmeg. Pour into the prepared pastry case, smooth the top and bake on the grid shelf on the floor of the roasting oven at 375°F (190°C) for 35–40 minutes. This flan may also be baked at the top of the baking oven in a 4-oven Aga. Serve hot or cold.

110g (4oz) wholemeal flour
110g (4oz) medium oatmeal
25g (1oz) sesame seeds
pinch salt
50g (2oz) margarine
50g (2oz) lard or white vegetable fat
2-3 × 15ml sp (2–3tbsp) water

Filling:
450g (1lb) fresh or frozen spinach
1 × 15ml sp (1tbsp) vegetable oil
1 bunch spring onions, trimmed and chopped
225g (8oz) curd cheese
2 eggs
50g (2oz) cheddar cheese, grated
150ml (¼pt) milk
salt and pepper
pinch grated nutmeg

Coronation Chicken

1 Wash the chickens and remove giblets. Place the chickens in one or two saucepans, add the sliced onion and carrot, bay leaf and seasoning and cover with cold water. Bring to the boil, cover and either simmer on the simmering plate for 50–60 minutes or place on the bottom of the roasting oven for the same time. The chickens may also be poached slowly in the simmering oven for 2–3 hours. Test a thigh or leg with a skewer; the juices should run clear when the flesh is cooked. Remove the chickens from the liquid (reduce the liquid and use for stock, soups etc) and cool.
2 Fry the chopped onion gently in the oil for 2 minutes (do not brown). Stir in the curry powder and cook for a further 1 minute. Add the pared lemon rind, 30ml (2tbsp) of the juice, tomato purée and red wine and simmer uncovered for about 5 minutes or until the sauce is reduced to about 50ml (2fl oz). Strain through a sieve and cool.
3 Sieve the mango chutney if the pieces of mango are large, then stir into the curry sauce. Add the mayonnaise and yoghurt, beating well to blend evenly. The sauce should now be of a thin coating consistency and straw coloured. Adjust seasoning, cover and refrigerate until required – not more than 2–3 days.
4 Boil the rice in salted water for 20–30 minutes. Drain and cool. Stir in the sultanas and nuts and arrange round the edge of a large serving plate. (The rice mixture may be cooked in advance and refrigerated or frozen.)
5 Remove the flesh from the chickens, discarding skin and bones. Cut the flesh into bite-sized pieces and place in a large bowl. Pour over the curry-flavoured mayonnaise and stir gently to coat. Spoon into the centre of the serving plate and decorate with watercress and slices of lemon.

2 × 1.5kg (3lb) oven-ready chickens
1 onion, sliced
1 carrot, sliced
1 bay leaf
salt and pepper
1 small onion, finely chopped
1 × 15ml sp (1tbsp) vegetable oil
4 × 5ml sp (4tsp) curry powder
1 lemon
1 × 15ml sp (1tbsp) tomato purée
150ml (¼pt) red wine
2 × 15ml sp (2tbsp) mango chutney
300ml (½pt) mayonnaise
150ml (¼pt) natural yoghurt
450g (1lb) long-grain brown rice
100g (4oz) sultanas
100g (4oz) unsalted peanuts or cashew nuts
watercress and lemon slices to garnish

1.5kg (3lb) cooked beetroot,
  peeled and finely chopped
450g (1lb) green or yellow
  courgettes, thinly sliced
6 spring onions, chopped
6×15ml sp (6tbsp) natural
  yoghurt
3×15ml sp (3tbsp) olive oil
1×15ml sp (1tbsp) cider vinegar
1×2.5ml sp (½tsp) mustard
  powder
1 clove garlic
salt and pepper

340g (12oz) sprouted mung beans
  (or any other sprouted bean or
  seed)
1 red pepper, seeded and chopped
1 yellow pepper, seeded and
  chopped
½ cucumber, chopped
175g (6oz) chinese cabbage
  leaves, finely chopped
4 sticks celery, chopped
1×15ml sp (1tbsp) cider vinegar
4×15ml sp (4tbsp) soya or
  sunflower oil
1×1.25ml (¼tsp) freshly grated
  root ginger
1×5ml sp (1tsp) tamari or soy
  sauce
salt and pepper
75g (3oz) cashew nuts
  to garnish

Beetroot and Courgette Salad

1 Place the cooked beetroot in a salad bowl with the courgettes and
  spring onion.
2 Place all the dressing ingredients in a screw-topped jar and shake
  vigorously. Pour over the vegetables and leave to marinate for at least
  1 hour before serving.

Sprouty Salad

1 Put the bean sprouts into a salad bowl and add the peppers, cucumber,
  chinese cabbage and celery.
2 Mix together all the dressing ingredients in a screw-topped jar and
  shake vigorously. Pour over the salad, mix well and garnish with the
  cashew nuts.

Tabbouleh

1 Mix the bulgar wheat with the salt, pour over the boiling water and leave to stand for 10–15 minutes until all the water has been absorbed and the wheat has puffed up.

2 Mix together the oil, lemon juice, mint, garlic, parsley or coriander and onion and pour over the soaked bulgar. Leave overnight in a refrigerator or cool place to marinate.

3 Next day, fold in the tomatoes and cucumber and spoon into a serving bowl.

200g (7oz) bulgar wheat
1×5ml sp (1tsp) salt
340ml (12fl oz) boiling water
50ml (2fl oz) olive oil
50ml (2fl oz) lemon juice
2×15ml sp (2tbsp) fresh chopped mint
2 cloves garlic, crushed
6×15ml sp (6tbsp) freshly chopped parsley or coriander
1 spanish or red onion, finely chopped
450g (1lb) tomatoes, chopped
½ cucumber, diced

Rum Babas (*makes 10 babas*)

1 In a bowl, blend together the yeast, milk and 50g (2oz) of the flour until smooth. Leave to stand in a warm place until frothy (about 20 minutes for fresh yeast, 30 minutes for dried).

2 Add the remaining flour, sugar, eggs, butter and currants and beat thoroughly for 3–4 minutes. This helps to develop the dough so that it will rise well.

3 Grease ten 8.5cm (3½in) ring moulds with white fat. Half fill the tins with the baba dough, cover with oiled polythene to prevent a skin forming and leave to rise in a warm place until the moulds are two-thirds full.

4 Bake near the top of the roasting oven at 400°F (200°C) for 15–20 minutes. Allow to cool for a few minutes then turn out onto a wire rack placed over a tray to catch the drips of syrup.

5 Warm the honey and water together and add rum to taste. While the babas are still hot, spoon over sufficient syrup to soak each baba well. Babas are difficult to serve if you pour over too much syrup initially as they become wet while standing so serve any extra syrup separately.

6 Heat the jam and water together, sieve it and use to glaze each baba. Leave to cool completely.

7 Pipe a whirl of cream into each baba with a large star nozzle and top with a cherry. Transfer carefully to a serving plate.

25g (1oz) fresh yeast or 1×15ml sp (1tbsp) dried yeast
6×15ml sp (6tbsp) warm milk
225g (8oz) plain strong flour
25g (1oz) caster sugar
4 eggs, beaten
110g (4oz) butter, soft but not melted
110g (4oz) currants
white fat for greasing
4×15ml sp (4tbsp) clear honey
4×15ml sp (4tbsp) water
rum
3×15ml sp (3tbsp) apricot jam
2×15ml sp (2tbsp) water
300ml (½pt) double or whipping cream, whipped
glacé cherries

Strawberry Meringue Torte

1 Sift flour and baking powder together. Cream the butter with 75g (3oz) of the sugar until light and fluffy. Beat in the egg yolks a little at a time, then beat in the vanilla essence. Fold in the flour mixture together with the milk, mix well and spread into 2 greased, floured and base-lined 20cm (8in) sandwich tins. (The mixture will be spread very thinly.)

2 Whisk the egg whites until stiff and whisk in the remaining sugar a little at a time until the meringue stands in stiff peaks.

3 Spoon the meringue into a large piping bag fitted with a large star

100g (3½oz) plain flour
2×5ml sp (2tsp) baking powder
75g(3oz) butter
250g (9oz) caster sugar
3 eggs, separated
1×2.5ml sp (½tsp) vanilla essence
6×15ml sp (6tbsp) milk
110g (4oz) flaked almonds
300ml (½pt) double cream, whipped
225g (8oz) fresh strawberries

–102–
CHRISTMAS DINNER
Creamy baked prawns
Roast turkey
Chestnut stuffing
Bacon twists
Cranberry sauce
Bread sauce
Christmas pudding
Rum or brandy sauce
Walnut butter
Brandy butter
Bombe noël
Rosy red fruit salad
Meringue whirl mince pies

nozzle and pipe a layer of stars over each sponge. Sprinkle with the flaked almonds and bake at 350°F (180°C) in the centre of the baking oven, or on the grid shelf at the bottom of the roasting oven protected by the cold solid shelf for 30–35 minutes. Do not leave any longer than this or the sponges will become dry and tough.

4   Leave to cool in the tins for 10 minutes, then place one sponge, meringue side up, on a serving plate. Spread with the cream, cover with the strawberries (cut in half if large) then top with the remaining sponge, meringue side up.

CHRISTMAS DINNER

Creamy Baked Prawns

340g (12oz) peeled prawns
black pepper
300ml (½pt) fromage frais
75g (3oz) fresh breadcrumbs
  (brown or white)
75g (3oz) butter
6 whole prawns to garnish

1   Butter 6 ramekin dishes and divide the prawns between them. Season thoroughly with the black pepper.
2   Cover with the fromage frais and sprinkle a layer of breadcrumbs over each one. Dot with the butter.
3   Bake at 375°F (190°C) at the bottom of the roasting oven or the top of the baking oven for 10 minutes. Finish off by placing in a roasting tin hung on the top set of runners in the roasting oven and grilling for 1–2 minutes or until the breadcrumbs are golden brown.
4   Serve garnished with the whole prawns.

Roast Turkey *colour opposite*

5.5kg (12lb) oven-ready turkey
1 onion, peeled
1 orange or lemon
50g (2oz) butter
600–750ml (1–1¼pt) turkey
  stock made with the giblets

1   Prepare and truss the turkey. Remove the wishbone and fill the breast end with Chestnut Stuffing. Place the onion and orange or lemon inside the cavity.
2   Smear the turkey liberally with the butter, then set in a large roasting tin. Pour round half the stock and cover the top with a sheet of foil.
3   Roast at 400°F (200°C) or as near to the top of the oven as possible for about 15 minutes per 450g (1lb) plus 15 minutes, basting occasionally. Larger birds should be cooked for 12 minutes per 450g (1lb) plus 12 minutes. Add more stock as the liquid in the roasting tin evaporates.
4   Remove the sheet of foil 35–40 minutes before the end of the cooking time to brown the bird well. Move the roasting tin to the lowest set of runners so that potatoes and parsnips may be roasted above.
5   Test to see if the turkey is cooked by piercing the thickest part of the thigh and drumstick with a skewer; any liquid should be clear.
6   Transfer the turkey to a carving plate, cover with foil and place in the simmering or warming oven or place on a tea towel on top of the simmering plate's insulated lid, for up to 30 minutes before carving.

Roast Turkey with Cranberry Sauce – page 104, Bread Sauce – page 104 (Kenwood)

Chestnut Stuffing

1   Fry the onion and chopped turkey liver in the butter until this has been absorbed.

2   Mix together the chestnut purée and the sausage meat and blend in the contents of the frying pan together with the remaining ingredients. Use to fill the breast end of the turkey.

1 onion, finely chopped
turkey liver
25g (1oz) butter
225g (8oz) chestnut purée
225g (8oz) sausage meat
1 small cooking apple, peeled and grated
2 sticks celery, grated
50g (2oz) sultanas
1×2.5ml sp (½tsp) thyme
salt and pepper
1 egg
1×15ml sp (1tbsp) fresh chopped parsley
1–2×15ml sp (1–2tbsp) brandy

225g (8oz) lean back bacon, rinded

Bacon Twists

1 Cut each rasher into half crosswise then again lengthwise making 3 or 4 small strips out of each rasher.
2 Twist each strip into a corkscrew and arrange them in rows on a baking sheet. Put skewers across the ends of the rows to hold the twists in place.
3 Bake at 400°F (200°C) or near the top of the roasting oven for 15–20 minutes or until crisp. Drain well and serve.

450g (1lb) cranberries
300ml (½pt) water
225g (8oz) demerara sugar

Cranberry Sauce *colour page 103*

1 Place the cranberries in a saucepan with the water and bring to the boil. Simmer for 20–25 minutes until soft and the skins begin to pop.
2 Add the sugar and simmer for a further 20 minutes. Store the preserve in sterilised jars until required.

1 medium onion, finely chopped
1 bay leaf
6 black peppercorns
1 × 1.25ml sp (¼tsp) mace
pinch salt
450ml (¾pt) milk
75g (3oz) freshly made white breadcrumbs
50g (2oz) butter
2 × 15ml sp (2tbsp) double cream

Bread Sauce *colour page 103*

1 Place the onion, bay leaf, peppercorns, mace and pinch of salt in the milk and leave to infuse in a warm place (eg on a tea towel on top of the simmering plate's insulated lid) for about 2 hours.
2 Over a low heat, bring the milk slowly to the boil, then strain.
3 Stir in the breadcrumbs and 25g (1oz) of the butter. Place the pan over a low heat and cook, stirring now and then, until the crumbs have swollen and thickened the sauce.
4 Just before serving, beat in the remaining butter and the cream and taste to check the seasoning.

225g (8oz) shredded suet
110g (4oz) self-raising flour (brown or white)
225g (8oz) breadcrumbs (brown or white)
1 × 5ml sp (1tsp) mixed spice
1 × 1.25ml sp (¼tsp) ground cinnamon
450g (1lb) soft brown sugar
225g (8oz) sultanas
340g (12oz) stoned raisins
450g (1lb) currants
50g (2oz) almonds, blanched, skinned and chopped
50g (2oz) mixed peel
1 apple, peeled, cored and chopped
1 carrot, scrubbed and grated
grated rind of 1 orange and 1 lemon
4 eggs
150ml (¼pt) stout
150ml (¼pt) barley wine
4 × 15ml sp (4tbsp) rum

Christmas Pudding *colour page 107*

1 In a bowl mix together the suet, flour, breadcrumbs, spices and sugar.
2 Gradually mix in the fruits, nuts and peel, followed by the apple, carrot and orange and lemon rind.
3 In a separate bowl beat together the eggs, stout, barley wine and rum. Empty over the dry ingredients and stir very well – more stout may be needed, particularly if using brown flour and crumbs, but the mixture should be of a dropping consistency. After mixing, cover the bowl and leave overnight.
4 Grease 2 × 1 litre (2pt) or 4 × 600ml (1pt) pudding basins and pack the mixture into them right to the top. Cover each basin with greaseproof paper and either a pudding cloth or a piece of foil; tie round the rims with string.
5 Stand each basin in boiling water to half the height of the basin and cook on the simmering plate for 1½ hours. Transfer to the simmering oven overnight. Remove the paper and cloths or foil and replace with clean ones.
6 To reheat, stand in boiling water to half the height of the basin and cook on the simmering plate for 30 minutes before transferring to the simmering oven for 1½ hours.

Rum or Brandy Sauce

40g (1½oz) butter
40g (1½oz) plain flour
450ml (¾pt) milk
40g (1½oz) caster sugar
2–3×15ml sp (2–3tbsp) rum or
  brandy

1 Place the butter, flour and milk in a saucepan and cook over a low heat, stirring all the time, until the sauce thickens and is smooth.
2 Stir in the sugar and cook over a low heat for 5 minutes, stirring all the time to prevent sticking.
3 Add the rum, then taste to see if more sugar or rum is needed before serving.

Walnut Butter

340g (12oz) unsalted butter
175g (6oz) light soft brown sugar
1×15ml sp (1tbsp) brandy
1×1.25ml sp (¼tsp) ground
  nutmeg
110g (4oz) walnut pieces, finely
  crushed

1 Beat together all the ingredients; except the walnuts; until smooth.
2 Fold in the crushed walnuts and spoon into a bowl for serving.

Note: Packed in a lidded container, this butter will store well in a deep freeze. Delicious served with Christmas Pudding.

Brandy Butter

175g (6oz) unsalted butter
175g (6oz) light soft brown sugar
grated rind of ½ orange
2–3×15ml sp (2–3tbsp) brandy

1 Cream the butter until creamy and white.
2 Gradually beat in the sugar and orange rind, then the brandy, a little at a time. Transfer to a bowl and chill until solid.

Bombe Noël

110g (4oz) glacé cherries, halved
110g (4oz) raisins
50g (2oz) no-soak dried apricots,
  roughly chopped
50g (2oz) crystallized pineapple,
  (optional)
25g (1oz) candied whole peel,
  chopped
3×15ml sp (3tbsp) brandy
3×15ml sp (3tbsp) grand
  marnier
25g (1oz) walnut pieces
25g (1oz) hazelnuts
25g (1oz) flaked almonds
3 egg yolks
75g (3oz) caster sugar
300ml (½pt) single cream
vanilla essence
150ml (¼pt) double cream,
  whipped
sugar-frosted holly to decorate

1 Place the fruit and candied peel in a bowl, stir in the brandy and grand marnier. Chop the walnuts and hazelnuts and sprinkle over the fruits, together with the flaked almonds – do not stir into the fruits. Cover and leave in a cool place for 2–3 hours to soak.
2 Beat together the egg yolks and sugar until creamy. Bring the single cream slowly to the boil on the simmering plate, then pour onto the egg mixture, stirring vigorously. Pour into a basin over a pan of simmering water and stir until thickened. Strain into a bowl, add the vanilla essence and cool.
3 Fold the double cream into the custard. Pour into a rigid container, cover and freeze for 2 hours.
4 Remove from the freezer, stir well and mix in the fruit and nut mixture with the brandy and grand marnier. Turn into a 1.5 litre (2¾pt) icecream bombe mould or pudding basin and freeze until firm.
5 Dip the basin into cold water and turn the bombe out onto a chilled serving plate (smooth the surface if necessary). Serve crowned with a sprig of sugar-frosted holly.

1 large orange
4 cloves
225g (8oz) blackcurrants
225g (8oz) redcurrants
225g (8oz) cranberries or cherries
110g (4oz) sugar
150ml (¼pt) water
225g (8oz) raspberries
450g (1lb) pears, peeled, cored
  and sliced

175g (6oz) plain flour
75g (3oz) butter
grated rind of 1 lemon
2 egg yolks
water to mix if needed
225g (8oz) mincemeat
2 egg whites
110g (4oz) caster sugar

–106–
FIREWORK PARTY
Bacon-wrapped sausages
Jacket potatoes
Minestrone soup
Plaited cheese and herb loaf
Wassail
Hot apple punch
Gingerbread squares

450g (1lb) pork chipolata sausages
450g (1lb) thick butcher's
  sausages
450g (1lb) streaky bacon

Large baking potatoes, allow 1 per
person for adults, ½ for children
oil for brushing
butter and grated cheese

Christmas Pudding – page 104
(Kenwood)

Rosy Red Fruit Salad

1 Peel the orange and place the rind in a pan with the cloves, currants, cranberries, sugar and water. Cover and simmer for 15–20 minutes or until all the fruit is tender but still whole.
2 Turn into a bowl, remove rind and cloves, add remaining fruit and chill thoroughly.

Meringue Whirl Mince Pies

1 Sift the flour into a bowl and rub in the butter until the mixture resembles fine breadcrumbs. Stir in the lemon rind. Add the egg yolks and enough water (if needed) to bind to a soft but not sticky dough. Chill.
2 Roll out pastry on a lightly floured board and cut 12 circles using a 7.5cm (3in) fluted cutter. Line 12 patty tins with the pastry circles.
3 Divide the mincemeat between the pastry cases, then bake at 400°F (200°C) or in the centre of the roasting oven for 10 minutes.
4 Meanwhile, whisk the egg whites until stiff, then gradually whisk in the sugar until very stiff and glossy. Spoon the meringue into a piping bag fitted with a star nozzle and pipe a meringue whirl on top of each mince pie. Return to the oven for a further 5–10 minutes until the meringue is lightly browned.

FIREWORK PARTY

Bacon-Wrapped Sausages

1 Separate all the sausages. Rind the bacon rashers and stretch with the flat blade of a knife.
2 Wrap one rasher round each sausage and place in a large ovenproof dish or roasting tin with the ends of the bacon tucked underneath.
3 Bake at 400°F (200°C) or near the top of the roasting oven for 40–50 minutes or until golden brown.

Jacket Potatoes

1 Scrub the potatoes thoroughly and dry. Brush all over with oil and bake at 400°F (200°C) or in a roasting tin in the centre of the roasting oven for 1–1½ hours or until soft.
2 Cut a deep cross in the top of each potato (cut in half for children), fill with butter and serve with a bowl of grated cheese.

175g (6oz) golden syrup
50g (2oz) black treacle
3 × 15ml sp (3tbsp) orange
  marmalade
225g (8oz) butter or margarine
250g (9oz) plain wholemeal flour
1 × 5ml sp (1 level tsp) bicarbonate
  of soda
2 × 15ml sp (2tbsp) ground ginger
1 × 5ml sp (1tsp) ground
  cinnamon
50g (2oz) soft brown sugar
1 lemon, grated rind and juice
150ml (¼pt) milk
2 eggs

Gingerbread Squares

1. Weigh the syrup and treacle into a saucepan, add the marmalade and butter or margarine and heat gently on the simmering plate, stirring gently, until the mixture is evenly blended.
2. Place the flour, bicarbonate of soda, spices and sugar in a large bowl. Add the grated lemon rind and make a well in the centre.
3. Whisk together the milk and eggs, stir in 1 × 15ml sp (1tbsp) strained lemon juice and pour into the well in the dry ingredients together with the cooled syrup and marmalade mixture. Gradually beat in the flour.
4. Beat the mixture thoroughly (it should be very runny), then pour into a greased and lined 18cm (7in) square cake tin. Bake at 275°F (135°C) or in the simmering oven for 2–2½ hours until the gingerbread is well risen and just firm to the touch.
5. Cool slightly in the tin then turn out onto a wire rack and cool completely. Wrap the cold cake in greaseproof paper and foil and store in a cool place for at least 3 days. To serve, cut into generous squares.

Note: This cake may be frozen once matured. Thaw, wrapped, at room temperature. The brown flour gives this moist cake a crumbly texture. For a stickier result replace some or all of the flour with plain white flour.

TEA TIME

175g (6oz) butter
175g (6oz) caster sugar
3 eggs
225g (8oz) self-raising flour
2 × 15ml sp (2tbsp) milk
2 × 15ml sp (2tbsp) cocoa powder
2 × 15ml sp (2tbsp) hot water
1 × 2.5ml sp (½tsp) vanilla
  essence
icing sugar for dusting (optional)

*Farmhouse Mincemeat Cake –
page 116, Melting Moments –
page 114, Plaited Cheese and
Herb Loaf – page 108
(Photography 2000)*

Marble Cake

1. Well grease a 1.5 litre (2½pt) ring mould with butter.
2. Cream the butter and sugar together until light and fluffy. Add the eggs one at a time, beating between each addition. Lightly fold in the flour together with enough milk to give a soft dropping consistency and divide the mixture into two.
3. Dissolve the cocoa powder in the hot water and allow to cool.
4. Add the cool cocoa and water mixture to one part and carefully mix in thoroughly. Add the vanilla essence to the other half.
5. Place the mixture in the prepared tin in alternate spoonfuls until all the mixture has been used up. Now swirl through the mixture with a skewer – don't exaggerate the movement as this will result in a disappointing effect.
6. Bake at 350°F (180°C) in the centre of the baking oven or on the grid shelf at the bottom of the roasting oven protected by the cold solid shelf, for 40–45 minutes until well risen and spongy to the touch. Turn out and cool on a wire rack. Serve plain or with a dusting of sifted icing sugar.

225g (8oz) stoned dates
150ml (¼pt) rum or brandy
150ml (¼pt) apple juice
225g (8oz) wholemeal flour
2×5ml sp (2tsp) mixed spice
175g (6oz) butter
1 carrot, scrubbed and finely
  grated
4 eggs
175g (6oz) sultanas
175g (6oz) raisins
110g (4oz) glacé cherries

Sugar-Free Rich Fruit Cake

1   Roughly chop the dates and soak in the rum and apple juice for 12 hours. Liquidise with the rum and juice.
2   Mix the flour with the spice.
3   In a large mixing bowl cream the butter and beat in the carrot. Beat in the eggs alternately with the flour. Beat in the liquidised dates, sultanas, raisins and cherries (first soaked in hot water to remove the syrup, then dried).
4   Pour the mixture into a greased and lined 20cm (8in) round cake tin and bake at 300°F (150°C) or in the simmering oven for 3–4 hours until a skewer inserted in the centre comes out cleanly.
5   Allow the cake to cool in the tin for 15 minutes then turn out onto a wire rack to cool completely.

Note: Wrapped in clingfilm and stored in the refrigerator this type of cake will keep for up to 3 weeks. It can also be successfully frozen, and thawed at room temperature when needed.

50g (2oz) glacé cherries
175g (6oz) butter
50g (2oz) caster sugar
75g (3oz) plain wholemeal flour
75g (3oz) plain white flour
50g (2oz) ground rice
50g (2oz) sultanas

Cherry and Sultana Shortbread

1   Soak the cherries in hot water for a few minutes to remove excess syrup; drain, pat dry and roughly chop.
2   Cream together the butter and sugar, taking care not to overbeat.
3   Stir in the flours, ground rice, sultanas and prepared cherries and mix to a soft dough.
4   Press into a greased and base-lined 18cm (7in) shallow square cake tin or a 18cm (7in) diameter loose-bottomed flan tin and level the surface using a palette knife.
5   Bake at 375°F (190°C) on the grid shelf at the bottom of the roasting oven for 30–40 minutes or until golden brown and firm to the touch.
6   While warm, cut into squares, oblongs or triangles (wedges if using a flan tin). Carefully lift out of the tin and cool completely on a wire rack.

110g (4oz) butter or block
  margarine
225g (8oz) self-raising wholemeal
  flour
110g (4oz) light soft brown sugar
75g (3oz) walnut pieces, roughly
  chopped
50g (2oz) glacé cherries
2-3 ripe bananas, about 340g
  (12oz), mashed
150ml (¼pt) natural yoghurt
1 egg

Banana and Yoghurt Tea Loaf

1   Rub the fat into the flour; stir in the sugar and 50g (2oz) of the walnuts.
2   Soak the cherries in hot water for 1 minute to remove the syrup and dry on kitchen paper. Cut in half and add to the flour mixture.
3   Mix together the mashed banana, yoghurt and egg and add to the dry ingredients to form a fairly stiff dough. Spoon into a greased and lined 1kg (2lb) loaf tin. Level the surface and sprinkle with the remaining walnuts.
4   Bake at 350°F (180°C) in the centre of the baking oven or on the grid shelf on the base of the roasting oven protected by the cold solid shelf, for 1¼–1½ hours or until a skewer inserted in the centre comes out clean. Leave to cool in the tin for 15 minutes before turning out onto a wire rack to cool completely.

Chocolate and Almond Fingers

1 Mix together the flour, cocoa powder, sugar, sultanas and flaked almonds.
2 Cut up the Mars bar and place in a pan with the chocolate and the butter; heat gently until melted. Pour onto the dry ingredients and mix well.
3 Spread the mixture into a 18cm (7in) shallow square tin and bake at 375°C (190°C) at the top of the baking oven or at the bottom of the roasting oven on the grid shelf for 25 minutes. The top will still be soft to the touch.
4 Leave in the tin to cool and set, then cut into 12 fingers.

175g (6oz) self-raising flour
25g (1oz) cocoa powder
110g (4oz) caster sugar
110g (4oz) sultanas
50g (2oz) flaked almonds
1 Mars bar
50g (2oz) milk chocolate
110g (4oz) butter

Marmalade Cake

1 In a bowl combine the flour, baking powder and spice; rub in the butter until the mixture resembles fine breadcrumbs. Stir in the sugar and orange rind.
2 Mix together the orange juice, marmalade and eggs and pour over the dry ingredients, mixing well to ensure there are no dry patches.
3 Pour into a greased and lined 18cm (7in) round cake tin. Bake at 350°F (180°C) in the centre of the baking oven, on the grid shelf on the base of the roasting oven protected by the cold solid shelf, or in a cake baker in the roasting oven, for 45–50 minutes.
4 Leave to cool in the tin for 15 minutes before turning out onto a wire rack to cool completely. Peel off the paper when cold.

275g (10oz) plain wholemeal flour
2×5ml sp (2 level tsp) baking powder
1×5ml sp (1tsp) mixed spice
150g (5oz) butter
150g (5oz) demerara sugar
grated rind 2 oranges
2×15ml sp (2tbsp) orange juice
3×15ml sp (3tbsp) orange marmalade
2 eggs

110g (4oz) butter
110g (4oz) caster sugar
1 egg
175g (6oz) self-raising flour
50g (2oz) rolled oats

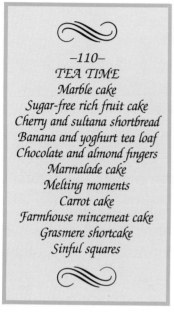

340g (12oz) soft brown sugar
3 eggs
175ml (6fl oz) sunflower oil
50ml (2½fl oz) plain yoghurt
2×5ml sp (2tsp) vanilla essence
1 orange, rind and ½ the juice
250g (9oz) plain wholemeal flour
1×5ml sp (1tsp) bicarbonate of
  soda
1×5ml sp (1tsp) nutmeg
1×2.5ml sp (½tsp) mixed spice
340g (12oz) carrots, grated
75g (3oz) desiccated coconut
110g (4oz) raisins

Topping:
225g (8oz) full fat soft cheese
75g (3oz) unsalted butter
110g (4oz) icing sugar
juice of ½ orange

Pickled Oranges – page 117,
French Apple Flan – page 36
(Photography 2000)

Melting Moments *colour page 111*

1   Cream together the butter and sugar until light and fluffy. Gradually beat in the egg, then fold in the flour to form a stiff dough.
2   Divide the mixture into 24 pieces, roll each piece into a ball the size of a walnut, then roll in the oats to cover completely.
3   Place on baking trays allowing room for them to spread; flatten slightly. Bake at 350°F (180°C) in the centre of the baking oven, or on the grid shelf on the base of the roasting oven protected by the cold solid shelf, for 15–20 minutes. Allow to set a little on the trays before removing to wire racks to cool.

Variations:
Omit the rolled oats, pipe the mixture through a round nozzle to give a gentle swirl and top each with half a glacé cherry before baking.
Chocolate melting moments: replace 15g (½oz) of the flour with 15g (½oz) cocoa powder and sift with the flour before using.
Ginger melting moments: add 1×5ml sp (1tsp) ground ginger to the flour before mixing into the other ingredients and place a small piece of candied ginger on top of each biscuit before baking.

Carrot Cake

1   In a mixing bowl place the sugar, eggs, oil, yoghurt, vanilla essence, orange rind and juice and beat together well.
2   Sift together flour, bicarbonate and spices, then add wet ingredients, followed by carrots, coconut and raisins. Mix well to distribute all the ingredients evenly, then spoon into a greased and lined 20cm (8in) deep round cake tin.
3   Bake at 300°F (150°C) for 1½–2 hours. For a 4-oven Aga bake in the baking oven. For any 2-oven cooker bake on the grid shelf on the floor of the roasting oven using the solid shelf to protect the cake. Once the top is set the cake may be transferred to the simmering oven for the remainder of the cooking time. Alternatively, bake in an Aga cake baker in the roasting oven. Leave to cool in the tin.
4   Mix topping ingredients together. Cut cake in half and use half the topping mixture to sandwich cake together, spread the other half thickly all over the top.

Note: This cake may be frozen, completed, then thawed in the refrigerator when required.

150g (5oz) butter or block margarine
150g (5oz) soft brown sugar
3 eggs
225g (8oz) self-raising wholemeal flour
1×5ml sp (1tsp) mixed spice
150ml (¼pt) apple juice
325g (11oz) mincemeat
50g (2oz) flaked almonds
75g (3oz) glacé cherries

Farmhouse Mincemeat Cake *colour page 111*

1 Cream together the butter and sugar until light and fluffy. Gradually beat in the eggs, one at a time.
2 Fold in the flour and mixed spice, followed by the apple juice, mincemeat, almonds and 50g (2oz) of the cherries.
3 Turn into a greased and lined 20cm (8in) diameter round cake tin and level the top. Decorate with a circle of the remaining cherries and bake at 350°F (180°C) in the centre of the baking oven or on the grid shelf on the base of the roasting oven protected by the solid shelf, for 1¼–1½ hours until firm to the touch and an inserted skewer comes out clean.
4 Leave in the tin to cool completely, then store in an airtight tin until required. This cake keeps well for 2 weeks in a tin but may also be frozen successfully.

275g (10oz) self-raising flour (white or brown)
2×5ml sp (2tsp) ground ginger
175g (6oz) butter
150g (5oz) soft brown sugar
grated rind of 1 lemon
110g (4oz) sultanas
1 egg
150ml (¼pt) milk

Filling:
50g (2oz) butter
175g (6oz) icing sugar
juice of 1 lemon

Grasmere Shortcake

1 Sieve together the flour and ginger and rub in the butter until the mixture resembles breadcrumbs.
2 Stir in the sugar, lemon rind and sultanas. Beat the egg and add to the mixture with enough milk to make a fairly stiff mixture (if a large egg is used use slightly less milk).
3 Turn the mixture into a greased and base-lined 21.5cm (8½in) diameter spring-clip tin and level the surface.
4 Bake the shortcake at 325°F (160°C), or on the grid shelf on the base of the roasting oven with the cold plain shelf on the top set of runners above, for 50 minutes. For the 4-oven Aga bake on the lowest set of runners in the baking oven for 50 minutes. The shortcake should be golden brown and firm to the touch.
5 To make the filling, cream together the butter, sugar and lemon juice until smooth.
6 When the cake is cold, carefully split in half and fill with the butter cream.

175g (6oz) butter
75g (3oz) caster sugar
225g (8oz) plain flour

Fudge:
110g (4oz) butter
110g (4oz) soft brown sugar
2×15ml sp (2tbsp) golden syrup
1×200g (7oz) can condensed milk

Topping:
175g (6oz) plain chocolate

Sinful Squares

1 Beat together the butter and caster sugar until fluffy then fold in the flour to form a stiff dough. Press into a greased 28×18cm (11×7in) swiss roll tin and bake at 375°F (190°C) or at the bottom of the roasting oven on the grid shelf for 10–15 minutes until firm to the touch and pale golden brown.
2 Place the butter, brown sugar, syrup and condensed milk in a pan and, once melted, boil gently for about 5 minutes stirring vigorously. Do not allow the mixture to burn. Pour onto the cooked shortbread and spread evenly with a palette knife. Cool completely.
3 Place the chocolate in a heatproof bowl over a pan of simmering water and stir until melted. Pour over the caramel and spread evenly. Chill until set. Cut into 24 equal squares.

WHAT ELSE?

Pickled Oranges *colour page 115*

6 large oranges
900ml (1½pt) cider vinegar
675g (1½lb) sugar
1×15ml sp (1tbsp) ground cloves
1 cinnamon stick

1   Slice oranges, put into a pan with sufficient water to cover and simmer on the simmering plate for about 45 minutes until the rind is really soft. Remove oranges with a slotted spoon.
2   Add the vinegar, sugar, ground cloves and cinnamon stick to the pan, bring to the boil and simmer for 10 minutes.
3   Add the oranges back to the pan and cook until the rind becomes transparent. Remove the oranges and pack them into sterilised jars.
4   Boil the syrup rapidly for a further 10 minutes to reduce it, then pour over the oranges. Seal immediately.

Note: Pickled oranges make a delicious accompaniment to cold meats, salads and curries.

Fresh Lime Curd

4 limes
3 eggs
75g (3oz) butter
110g (4oz) caster sugar

1   Finely grate the lime rinds and place in a bowl with the strained juice, eggs, fat and sugar.
2   Place the bowl over a pan of simmering water and whisk constantly until the curd thickens sufficiently to coat the back of the spoon – this may take 20 minutes.
3   Take off the heat and pour into sterilised jars; seal immediately and refrigerate for up to 3 weeks. This curd may also be frozen.

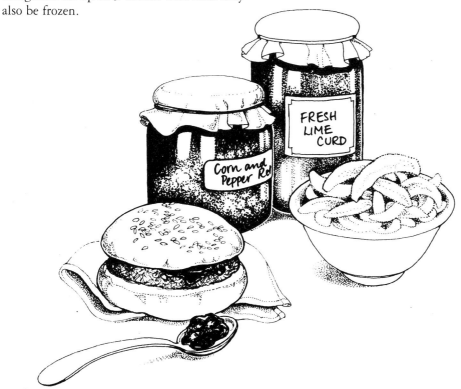

700g (1½lb) onions, chopped
850ml (1½pt) pickling
   vinegar
1kg (2lb) beans, weighed after
   trimming and slicing
1×15ml heaped sp (1 heaped
   tbsp) cornflour
1×15ml sp (1tbsp) dry mustard
   powder
1×15ml sp (1tbsp) turmeric
225g (8oz) soft brown sugar
450g (1lb) demerara sugar

Runner Bean Chutney

1   Put the chopped onions into a large pan or preserving pan with 300ml (½pt) of the vinegar. Bring to the boil and let them simmer gently for about 20 minutes or until onions are soft.
2   Meanwhile, blanch the sliced beans in boiling salted water for 5 minutes, strain and add to the onions.
3   In a basin mix cornflour, mustard powder and turmeric with enough of the remaining vinegar to make a smooth paste and then add to the onion mixture.
4   Pour in the rest of the vinegar and simmer everything for 10 minutes.
5   Stir in both the sugars over a gentle heat until they dissolve and continue to simmer for 1–1½ hours until thickened.
6   Pot the chutney in clean warm jars; seal and label when cold. Keep for at least a month before eating.

2×326g (11½oz) cans
   sweetcorn
2 green peppers, cored, seeded and
   chopped
1 red pepper, cored, seeded and
   chopped
1 onion, chopped
1 cucumber, chopped (do not peel)
4 tomatoes, chopped (do not peel)
300ml (½pt) cider vinegar
175g (6oz) light soft brown sugar
1×2.5ml sp (½tsp) salt
1×15ml sp (1tbsp) celery salt
1×15ml sp (1tbsp) mustard seed
1×5ml sp (1tsp) turmeric

Corn and Pepper Relish *(makes 1½–2kg: 3–4lb)*

1   Combine all the ingredients in a preserving pan or large saucepan. Bring to the boil and simmer for 25–30 minutes or until the vegetables are tender. If the relish has not thickened, boil rapidly for 5–10 minutes or until the excess liquid has been absorbed. Keep stirring to avoid the relish sticking and burning.
2   Pack into hot sterilised jars and seal immediately with jam covers and screw-top lids. The use of screw lids will prevent the relish drying out.

Note: This relish makes an ideal accompaniment to cold meats and also barbecue dishes. It should be stored in a cool place or refrigerator and used within 3–4 weeks.

3 oranges
3 lemons
1×5ml sp (1tsp) salt
water
450g (1lb) granulated sugar
175–225g (6–8oz) caster sugar

Candied Citrus Peel

1   Remove the peel with the pith from the fruit as neatly as possible and cut into 75mm (¼in) wide strips.
2   Place the peel in a pan with the salt and sufficient water to cover; bring to the boil. Simmer for about 20 minutes until the peel is tender (the lemon peel may take longer than the orange). Drain and rinse under cold water until cool, then drain well.
3   Dissolve the granulated sugar in 300ml (½pt) of water over the simmering plate, then bring to the boil. Add the peel and simmer gently for 40 minutes or until most of the syrup has been absorbed, the pith is pale yellow and the peel has turned transparent and glossy.
4   Remove the peel with a slotted spoon and shake off any excess syrup.
5   Roll the strips in some of the caster sugar then spread on baking sheets lined with baking parchment. Space the strips well apart so that they do not stick together. Place in the simmering oven at 225–250°F (110–120°C) for about 1 hour to dry. When dry, re-roll the strips of peel in more caster sugar and store in an airtight container ready for use.

Index